Shokoofeh Azar

THE ENLIGHTENMENT OF THE GREENGAGE TREE

Translated from the Persian

Europa
editions

Europa Editions
8 Blackstock Mews
London N4 2BT
www.europaeditions.co.uk

A catalogue record for this title is available from the British Library
ISBN 978-1-78770-310-0

Azar, Shokoofeh
The Enlightenment of the Greengage Tree

Book design by Emanuele Ragnisco
www.mekkanografici.com

Cover design: Debra Billison.
Paintings by Shookofeh Azar used for cover design: 1. The Poetry
Night; 2. Two Birds; 3. Red Bird and Moon

Prepress by Grafica Punto Print – Rome

Printed and bound in Great Britain by Clays Ltd, Elcograf S.p.A.

We are not the first people to have destroyed ourselves;
with a city where all devices of felicity were present.
—"Manifest of Desolation" by BAHRAM BEIZAI

Dedicated to all those I know: dead and alive.

THE
ENLIGHTENMENT
OF THE
GREENGAGE TREE

CHAPTER 1

Beeta says that Mom attained enlightenment at exactly 2:35 P.M. on August 18, 1988, atop the grove's tallest greengage plum tree on a hill overlooking all fifty-three village houses, to the sound of the scrubbing of pots and pans, a ruckus that pulled the grove out of its lethargy every afternoon. At that very moment, blindfolded and hands tied behind his back, Sohrab was hanged. He was hanged without trial, and unaware he would be buried *en masse* with hundreds of other political prisoners early the next morning in a long pit in the deserts south of Tehran, without any indication or marker lest a relative come years later and tap a pebble on a headstone and murmur *there is no god but God*.[1]

Beeta says Mom came down from the tallest greengage tree and, without looking at Beeta who was filling her skirt with sour greengages, walked towards the forest saying, "This whole thing is not at all as I'd thought." Beeta wanted Mom to explain, but Mom, as though mesmerized like someone with forest fever—what I call *forest melancholia*—walked with a steady step and hollow gaze into the forest to climb up the tallest oak where she sat on its highest bough for three days and three nights in the sun, rain, moonlight, and fog, looking with bewilderment at the life she was seeing for the first time.

---

[1] In Iranian culture it is common to tap a small stone against the headstone and say "there is no god but God." The tapping is to wake the spirit of the dead to hear the recital of this phrase.

Just as Mom reached the highest branch, perched to view her own life, the complex lives of family both distant and near, the events of that big five-bedroom house in that five-hectare grove, Razan, Tehran, Iran, and then suddenly the whole planet and universe, Beeta ran to the house and announced that though still harboring a mania for fireflies, Mom also now had a mania for heights! At first none of us took her new infatuation seriously, but when midnight had come and gone and there was still no sign of her, first I, then Dad, then Beeta carrying a lantern, went and sat down under the tree. We lit a fire upon which we placed a zinc kettle so the fragrance of our smoked tea would fill the Jurassic-age Hyrcanian forest—the last of its kind—and lure Mom down. The fragrance of the northern-smoked tea reached Mom's nostrils as she was traversing the Milky Way, watching the stars and planets spinning and orbiting with astonishing order, every rotation of which split open a space in which scientists hopelessly searched for a sign of God. From up there, perched on star dust, gazing down at an Earth no bigger than a tiny speck, she came to the same conclusion she had reached that day at precisely 2:35 P.M.: it's not worth it, life isn't what she had thought. Life is precisely that which she and others were prodigiously killing—the moment itself. A moment carrying in its womb the past and future; just like lines on the palm of one's hand, in the leaf of a tree, or in her husband, Hushang's eyes.

Around five o'clock the next morning, Dad, Beeta, and I woke up in the thick morning fog to see the last foxes returning to their dens after hunting Razan's chickens and roosters, and to feel the wings of the hoopoe just inches away. Mom had once again returned to the highest bough from her peregrination among the planets and cities, villages, islands, and tribes, in time to hear the song of thousands and thousands of sparrows, and to see a hedgehog curl up and roll down the forest slope because Dad had moved. We all took our places at the same time; us around the fire, Mom up in the tree, Sohrab in the pit alongside hundreds of other corpses. After all, the executioners were so overwhelmed, they had been unable to bury the bodies in time as planned. But the first killed were the lucky ones. In the following days, the number of people executed increased so much that corpses piled high in the prison back yard and began to stink, and Evin's ants, flies, crows, and cats, who hadn't had such a feast since the prison was built, licked, sucked and picked at them greedily. Juvenile political prisoners had the good fortune to be pardoned by the Imam if they fired the final shot that would put the condemned out of their misery. With bruised faces, trembling hands, and pants soaked with urine, hundreds of thirteen- and fourteen-year-olds, whose only crime had been participating in a party meeting, reading banned pamphlets, or distributing flyers in the street, fired the last shot into faces that were sometimes still watching them with twitching pupils.

It was mayhem, and the executioners were so overwhelmed by the stench of loathsome death that filled the hall that they would go sporadically mad and be transferred directly to a military asylum, only to vanish or be killed months later. From July 29, 1988, when the first series of executions of the People's Mojahedin and communist prisoners began, until mid September of the same year when more than five thousand people in Tehran, Karaj, and other cities were hanged or shot by firing squad, only three provincial soldiers disobeyed firing orders. Their bodies, along with those executed, became eternal hosts to three lead bullets. Midway through the second month, of the dozens of refrigerated-semi drivers, whose job had been to haul bodies to the remote desert outside the city, four also ended up in the asylum. The stench of putrefied bodies had so clogged their nostrils, they thought it emanated from them wherever they went, and gave them away. They suspected their wives could smell it, too, but didn't let on, out of pity or fear. They were frightened of the apprehensive looks they received when standing in the long line for food ration coupons, bread, or pasteurized milk. One of them thought the black crows gathering in ever greater numbers around the corpse-filled trenches were stalking him. He thought the stench of his own body had brought the crows to break him: now sitting on house walls, perched on the power poles, and flying above the city. In the smaller cities, two members of a firing squad, whose job had been to execute political prisoners in the desert outside the city, were shot in the back as they ran away from their duties. Meanwhile, due to their "excellence in carrying out duties," hundreds of executioners and putrefied-corpse transporters were promoted to become Revolutionary Guards, interrogators, mayors, retribution executors, and prison wardens.

When Dad called out with his cheery morning voice that it was time for tea with *kondak* bread, he was sure Mom wasn't going to forget her latest craze. That's why he added hastily, "If there is one thing we inherited from our forefathers it's this mania; a mania for new things. For impossible things." Then gradually the morning fog got thicker and thicker, blurring out the three of us, with our lantern, fire and teakettle; and allowing Mom another opportunity to travel through a world that contained a planet which, despite all its vastness and countries and religions and books and wars and revolutions and executions and births and this oak tree, she had just realized was nothing but a minuscule speck in the universe.

At the age of forty-four, Mom suddenly became old. Her hair turned grey and Beeta, who was the first one in the house to see her in three days, yelled, "An old woman just arrived!" When Dad and I ran to see her, Mom had positioned herself on the living-room couch and was filing her left thumbnail with mysterious calm.

Mom's three-day enlightenment in the tree suddenly gave me an idea. Mom had just begun filing her right thumbnail when I gathered all my books from the bookcase. Smiling at all of them, I told them that if something went missing from the house, to know it was I who had taken it. Then, to an astonished look from Beeta, Mom's otherworldly stare, and Dad's usual smirk, without a backward glance, I went to Dad's workroom and grabbed what I needed: a hammer, nails, saw, and twine. It took five days to build my treehouse the way I wanted, that is, where it couldn't be seen, at the highest point of the tallest oak tree in the forest—the same tree that, until an hour ago, was the site of Mom's ascension. It had a window facing the sunrise and a door facing its setting, with a small balcony facing the house, and a rope railing. A big tarp covered the roof and all the branches, so that on rainy days and nights it would produce the same sound I had loved all thirteen years of my life; a tarp that every summer, prior to Sohrab's arrest, was spread out over the wooden shelves and cellar floor for silkworm production. There the worms spent a full two weeks eating mulberry leaves till, dreaming of butterflies, they spun their cocoons and then, unbeknownst to them, were drowned and boiled in a big vat. From their cocoons, white silk threads would be spun that only *some* of the wealthy carpet sellers in the cities of Isfahan, Nain and Kashan could afford. They gave this silk thread to destitute carpet weavers who couldn't leave their dank basements for even a minute during the day to greet the sun. They only knew one thing: how to weave silkworm dreams.

Sitting on the green sofa across from Mom and looking at her absently filing her nail, Dad thought that although he, a skilled *tar* player, was the source of the family's silkworm production and indisputable heir of the ability to interact with supernatural creatures, he had never been fortunate enough to see Mom in flight.

When Dad saw Mom for the first time heading down to Darband Park, she was barely seventeen and in the throes of an impossible love; a love that, for the first and last time, allowed her to soar over Naser Khosrow Street, over passersby and second-hand booksellers. Just six months before meeting Dad, she had had another, significantly more exhilarating, encounter, but one without a future. It was so exhilarating that from then on, and for the rest of her life, she heaved sighs like no other. They were long and deep and as concealed as possible, but not to the extent that in all those years, Dad hadn't noticed. At twenty-five, Dad fell so intensely in love with Mom—Roza—and at first sight, that at the end of that very same day, a night among Darband's foggy nights, he married her, in a daze and in the presence of a passing mullah who, fearful of dark specters and fog, was muttering prayers as he rushed, oil lamp in hand, down the slope. Having received his twenty tomans and a tip, the mullah didn't even linger long enough to behold the young couple's passionate first kiss. Dad placed a dogwood berry in Mom's mouth and said, "Let's go and introduce you to my family."

Despite all of Mom and Dad's strange qualities, my favorite family member is my father's little brother, Khosrow. As I was building my treehouse I recalled that he was able to turn any task into a mystical ritual. The second of three children, each born three years apart, he had proven himself to be the most befitting heir to the family mania. He spent a year in prison under Mohammad Reza Shah, two years under Khomeini; married, divorced; spent three years in self-imposed exile at home to study seventy-nine volumes of Indian and East Asian mysticism and learn Sanskrit. After spending three days and nights lying in an empty grave in a Tibetan cemetery reading the Vedas, he levitated one meter above the ground while practicing Osho meditation; he lived for a month in a wooden boat in the middle of a Siberian lake, as instructed by a shaman.

While weaving a branch in and out of the others to form a wall for my treehouse and thinking about Uncle Khosrow's craziness, I was overcome by a moment of despair—there was nothing new and different left in the world for me to do. We had to wait for Uncle Khosrow because in any case it was he who was the most likely to understand Mom. He was an experienced searcher, the exact opposite of me and us. We were just beginning.

As I was building my treehouse and thinking about all Uncle Khosrow had done, and Mom's unexpected enlightenment and ascension atop the greengage and oak trees, a surprise summer rain began to fall that continued for three days and nights. It would have turned me into a scaly, reptilian creature that feeds on algae, rotten fruit, and moss if Beeta, like a fallen angel with her orange umbrella and pleated sky-blue skirt, hadn't appeared to take me back into the house. At sunset on the fifth day, in the silence of the grove and awaiting the arrival of Uncle Khosrow, or news of Sohrab, my treehouse was completed.

CHAPTER 2

T hey say you are always waiting for someone, but when that person finally arrives it's not who you were expecting. Turan, my forty-something-year-old aunt, and her six grown and half-grown children are panting their way up the hill to the grove. They don't see me watching them from the window in my little forest house, hidden in the thick oak foliage. Very young, at seventeen or eighteen, Aunt Turan married a forty-year-old man from an established Isfahani family and proceeded to give birth to baby after baby. Now at least fifty kilos overweight, she's hauling herself up the hill like a snorting animal. Her six lazy, imbecile children are huffing along behind her like a pulsating steam train, hanging off one another and making faces, breaking branches and eating fruit behind her. Like a six-headed monster they ascend the hill and ravage the grove in a fraction of a second. Beeta, sitting as usual under one of the greengage trees, sees them and runs towards them yelling, both in greeting and to warn the residents of the house of the arrival of the aunt everyone prays will soon leave.

Mom and Dad each emerged from a different corner of the five-bedroom house, Mom immediately thinking of the seven extra mouths to feed, and Dad that he needed to lock his workroom door. Beeta thought about where to hide her pink leotard and ballet slippers, and I that I should conceal the rest of my things in the house. From the three local workers dragging up their heavy suitcases, it was clear the grove would be under their control for the foreseeable future. Before even reaching the house, the children had left a trail of destruction in their wake, while Aunt Turan, scolding them under her breath, endeavored to enter their hosts' house honor intact. Before even crossing the full length of the yard, Aunt Turan had shared, with much bravado, the news from the big Tehran clan, completely unconscious of the fact that, with Sohrab's arrest, these endless updates didn't interest Mom and Dad in the least.

Shahriyar, Dad's second cousin on his father's side, who had a PhD in economics and was expelled from university for his socialist leanings during the cultural revolution and now drives a long-haul taxi between Tehran and Isfahan had, as usual, had an accident, that had instantly killed his four passengers. This was the fifth time that Death had been found loitering around Dad's second cousin but from whom he had escaped unscathed. Aunt Turan reported that once, after this accident, upon reaching Isfahan, Shahriyar noticed one of his passengers didn't get out. He looked at him inquiringly in the rearview mirror. As soon as Shahriyar saw the cold, quiet face of the man in black he recognized him. That is why, without a word, he simply picked up another fare and drove back to Tehran. In the middle of the night, once all his passengers had left and the man in black was still sitting there, Shahriyar looked at him in the mirror and said, "Sir, I see I've reached the end of my line!" He held his car key out towards the man. The man in black said, "I see you know who I am!" According to Aunt Turan, Shahriyar told the man he spent so much time thinking about him from morning to night that he had recognized him as soon as he had set eyes upon him.

When Aunt Turan noticed that, for the first time, something she had said had sparked Mom and Dad's interest, she cut herself off spitefully and, still walking, said, "Well, I'll keep it short . . . Shahriyar thought Death had come to take his soul, but in fact he had only come to tell him not to despair; he wasn't going to bother him."

Crossing the yard and panting under her one-hundred-and-twenty kilos, Aunt Turan said that since that had happened, nobody in the family would get in the car with Shahriyar, even for a second, because it was clear he'd made a deal with Azrael, the Angel of Death. She said his wife and child had left him because they thought he was cursed and were fearful also that the neighbors' reproach might extend to them as well. But even then, he didn't pay any attention, saying Death treats everyone differently.

Aunt Turan related the story correctly but was unaware of many details. For instance, she didn't know that, upon seeing that the man didn't leave the taxi, Shahriyar, who had moved from depression to alcohol after the universities were purged, hit the accelerator and set off towards Shahran Heights, from which point Tehran's lights sparkled like diamonds. Then, once he had made sure no one was around, he pulled out two shot glasses and a flask of liquor from under his seat, and still seated behind the wheel with the stranger in the back, he filled both, handed one to the stranger and said, "To what is written and cannot be rewritten!" Before the stranger could open his mouth, Shahriyar drank two shots, turned to him and said, "Now I'm totally ready, Sir!" Impressed with Shahriyar's magnanimity, Death drank his glass and listened as Shahriyar said, "I always wanted to die in this exact spot with Tehran in all of its filth and beauty at my feet." After a pause, he continued, "The other reason I always liked coming up here was to find the house of the woman I loved from among all the others." Then laughing loudly, he said, "But after years of watching the lights go on and off and thinking about love, I realized there were no women in my life that I loved."

But Death, who truly *had* come to take Shahriyar's soul, said to himself that he would let this man enjoy his last moments. That's why he asked Shahriyar to give him another shot of the liquor. Hearing this, Shahriyar laughed, got out of the car and pulled a four-liter jug of bootleg liquor from its hiding place by the spare wheel in the boot. Without saying a word, they clinked their glasses and proceeded to drink to one another's health, repeatedly, until they were blind drunk. Afterwards they ran towards the mountains in the dark, stripped naked, danced, sang, and spun their underwear around on their fingers. As Tehran, with all its mullahs and rich people and Hezbollahis and prostitutes and political prisoners and lovers and homeless people and poets, drifted off to sleep at their feet, they spread their legs slightly and began to urinate over it. Then they compared their members, laughed, and were so inebriated they fell to the ground right there and fell into a deep slumber. Several hours later when dawn's cool breeze gave them goosebumps, they awoke with a start. Despite the astringent taste of liquor still making his head spin, Death admitted that never in his life had he had so much fun. He then told Shahriyar that they should get back to the city and, as he was getting out at Shemiran Square, paying his fare despite Shahriyar's insistence otherwise, he said that Shahriyar needn't worry about death, anymore! Still drunk, he staggered away down Shariati Street in the fresh morning light, laughing out loud and touching his member which he had realized was much smaller than Shahriyar's.

Now, having lit a cigarette, Aunt Turan began talking about Shokoofeh, her first cousin once removed, whose fiancé, Shahram, had left her and gone to America. One day Shokoofeh fell asleep and woke up three days later, inquiring fearfully, "Where's Shahram?" When she realized she had slept for three days and three nights and had forgotten her fiancé had left her ages ago, she became frightened. Falling asleep that very night, she didn't wake up for a month and when she did, again she wondered fearfully where Shahram was. This time when she realized she had been asleep for a whole month and that her memory had become even shorter, she was afraid to sleep, so to stay awake, she cut her finger with a knife and rubbed salt into her eyes every night. However, after days of not sleeping, she fell asleep one night. Now it's been six months and sixteen days, and she still hasn't woken up to then, fearfully, ask, "Where's Shahram?"

Mom and Dad let out a sigh of pity for this first cousin once removed and, taking Aunt Turan by the shoulder, led her beneath the ceiling fan in the living room that was pushing the hot, midday summer air from side to side. It didn't cool. Utterly motionless, the air mourned the ominous and silent events of that accursed summer, the likes of which existed in neither conscious nor unconscious memories of any of the family's living members. Even Uncle Khosrow, who in those days did nothing but read history books to identify historical correlations in family events and write in the family tree, did not come across even a single line in any of the books covering the last two hundred years about a massacre like the one that happened that year.

After that event, and ever since our five-member family had moved from Tehran to this five-hectare grove in a distant village in Mazandaran, Aunt Turan was the first family member to make her way to us. Nobody knew or dared ask, "How?" because then she would immediately say, "If we're not welcome, we'll leave." However, it didn't take long for all of us to realize what she was up to, although by then it was already too late. Two weeks after their surprise arrival on a hot sunny day, Aunt Turan went swimming with her six children in a small pond in the middle of the forest and suddenly vanished, before our eyes.

In our family, it was Beeta who loved swimming and who was in the water with them, but when, in the blink of an eye the water and all seven of them disappeared into thin air, Beeta found herself flopping around in the slimy muck on the bottom of the pond, her face and body covered in mud, opening and closing her mouth in bewilderment like a tiny fish dying in the slime mouthing, "Water . . . water . . . water . . ."

That was the day I finally saw everyone actually frightened by one of the strange things that occurred in the family. Beeta screamed and ran into Mom's arms. Mom stared so long at where the pond and seven people had been that night fell, and Dad had to go with a lantern to bring her back. Having observed everything, I was silent, waiting to see if Beeta knew anything. Yes, she knew. She knew exactly. That night after Mom had put salt in her mouth and Beeta had finally come out of shock, she admitted having seen Aunt Turan go to the forest a number of times at sunset to talk and connive with invisible beings.

After that, little by little, some of Mom and Dad's books disappeared from their library. Then, a large mat that had been stashed, unused, under my bed vanished, and then an oil lantern, a plate, fork and spoon, a pot and some food, and then finally, a blanket. The day before, Sohrab's camera had disappeared from his desk. Mom, who had forgotten that I had warned her about this, attributed it to the invisible presence of Aunt Turan and her six children. Finally, she came into the living room one day and yelled angrily, "What on earth is going on in this house?" Scared, I quickly answered from my room, "I inherited Sohrab's camera!" Pulling off her ballet slippers, Beeta screamed, "Idiot! The way you say it makes it sound like he's been killed—executed!" The only one who knew of Sohrab's execution, I quickly jumped out my bedroom window with the last things I needed and ran to my treehouse. Although I had officially declared I was not responsible for more stealing, things continued to disappear and be moved around the house.

Some days, objects cheekily moved around right before our

eyes until one day things went so far that while we were all sitting around the table eating lunch, we could hear frenzied munching, and the stench of belches reached our noses. It couldn't be denied any longer because food was being lifted from our plates only to disappear into thin air to the sound of noisy chewing. If Dad hadn't put a stop to this excess on the part of Aunt Turan and her six gluttonous, ill-mannered children he might have had to bring in Razan's Soothsayer—a terrifying prospect for any jinn. After the First Soothsayer disappeared in Razan's fire, this Soothsayer was said to have emerged from the forest one day and come to Razan. At any rate, without a Soothsayer, Razan was unable to control the relations with, and excesses of, the invisible beings around the forest who were constantly trying to force their presence, preferences and laws on the people of the region.

One night while we were all talking, laughing, and eating sunflower seeds around a fire in the yard, Dad suddenly grabbed Aunt Turan's invisible wrist in mid-air, threatening that if she didn't leave us alone he would bring the Soothsayer to darken her days. Taken by surprise, a sunflower seed caught in her throat and Aunt Turan began to cough. Finally, she said, "It's your fault. You saw us as such a burden, so this is what happened to us. Now you have to put up with it." But Dad didn't give in and, squeezing her wrist, said, "Then it will be, as I said!" For a moment, Aunt Turan seemed to regret what she had done and with a sad, honest voice said, "Nobody wants us. We weren't even welcome in our own home. My stingy husband saw the children as rivals and bought a separate refrigerator for himself which he kept locked. Everywhere we went people soon began padlocking their refrigerators. So, this year I resolved to do it. I read one of Father's books on the secrets of relations with jinns. It was with their help that I found the way to your house. I came here to join them. Now I'm with them and I'm happy."

From then on we no longer heard Aunt Turan's children eating, or smelled her foul belches; but we were all deeply saddened by her story and promised ourselves not to react when things in the house were rearranged. Although we could no longer count on finding food in the refrigerator, which in those years was hard to come by, nobody complained. A mere three days later, word from the village had it that a troop of hungry jinns was ravaging Razan. The time had come for the Soothsayer. The villagers say that before he had even wiped the dust from his mirror or spoken a formula, the amateur jinns became frightened and chose flight over fight. Now occasional rumors from villages in distant forests complain of a hungry band of jinns that has wiped out food supplies.

For several months, nobody really knew about my treehouse. Then one day, with the usual pipe in his mouth as he was riding his brown horse aimlessly to the grove's far reaches, Dad caught sight of the rope ladder and, climbing up it, found my papers among the things swiped from the house, and began to read. That night at the table with everyone looking at their last bites, Dad pulled out a notebook and, not looking at me, began to read aloud: *Dad's hand-made tar was still in my hands when it happened. I don't have words to describe it. I'm trying to forget that horrible burning of my skin and eyeballs . . . I need to keep my mind busy with other things. I need to write. To think about them. About those who are now so alone.*

It felt as if my face and neck had flushed purple—I was so angry. I couldn't curse Dad. That just wasn't done in our family, but I really wanted to call him a shithead. It was the worst swear word I knew. Beeta said, "And?" Dad continued: *I need to write. I must remember to take that four-hundred-page notebook from Dad's room. When I write, I can better focus on distracting myself.*

Without finishing my meal, I ripped the notebook from

Dad's hands. It flew through the air and was sailing out the door when Mom said sternly, "You're growing up. You can't behave like that anymore." With my back still to them, I said insolently, "Have you forgotten? I'm not going to grow up!" As I was exiting the house, Mom repeated one of her favorite sayings, "I don't care if people's lives are divided into before Nowruz and after Nowruz, or before the Revolution and after the Revolution, but in my family, it's divided into before the Arab invasion and after the Arab invasion." After that event Mom always said *Arab invasion*, not *fire* or *burning*... She still insists on the fact that they came and burnt, plundered, and killed. Just like 1,400 years ago.

CHAPTER 3

Last winter when Mom hadn't yet been up in the green-gage tree, Sohrab hadn't yet been executed, and the events with Aunt Turan and her hungry children hadn't yet come to pass, by the time the five of us woke up to the barking of our guard dog, Gorgi, early on the rainy morning of February 6, 1988, it was already too late to help Sohrab run into the forest. In the blink of an eye, four armed Revolutionary Guards and a mullah descended on the house, snapped handcuffs on Sohrab who was still in bed and, grabbing randomly at some pamphlets and books, took him away. Before Dad could run after them or Mom could scream, "Where are you taking my son, you thugs?!" they sped away in their Patrols, mud from under the wheels splattering on our faces, as Gorgi continued to bark.

For five months, nobody knew where Sohrab was being held until one day a stranger with an unkempt face and sorrowful eyes entered Razan, and pointing to our house up on the hill to the first man he came across, said, "Tell them they can find their son in Evin prison." Just as he had come, the sad stranger set off along the winding alleyways towards the paths that led to the forest, to deliver prisoners' messages to other families. Before he could leave, however, a man sitting in one corner of the village square, sharpening his knife on a rock, said, "Why do you go to the trouble of delivering news to people you don't know?" The sad man said, "The story is much longer than you have patience for." And he set off again. But the villager went after him with slow, steady steps and handing him a hand-rolled cigarette, said, "I have lots of patience." It was thus that the stranger sat down across from the villager who was once again sharpening his knife, and said, "I grew up in a family that was so poor that eating chicken was our biggest dream. When I was just twelve, my mother fell pregnant again. One night I heard her tell my father that she was prepared to die for a chicken thigh. The next day I was thrown in jail for stealing a chicken, but I was content because, before being arrested, we were able to cook it for my mother, who ate its thigh with ecstatic pleasure. I was released a year later and was shocked to see my parents had both become ten years older, and poorer. When I was fifteen, I landed in prison again, this time for killing my boss because he wouldn't pay my wages. "Every day my longing to see my mother was greater than the day before, but not once did she come to visit me. Years passed. I was taken to the gallows six times but each time the rope snapped, so eventually, it was decided I would be released. Several days later, however, my little brother, the light of my parents' life, ended up in the same prison with me. No matter how much I asked, he wouldn't tell me his crime. Finally, in the middle of the night, the night guard whispered the story to me. He said my brother had killed all six of our brothers and sisters, and our parents. When I heard this, I went deaf and blind and slit the vein in my little brother's neck with a razor, right then and there, as he slept. He just had the chance to flash me a tearful smile. "The next day, the newspaper made it into the prison; the news passed from cell to cell, and from the prisoners' whispers, I learned the truth. My little brother, the only one of us children to go to school, had learned in science class that ether could be used to make people unconscious. That very night, he placed eight ether-soaked rags over the noses of everyone in the house as they slept, so he could go and sell cigarettes on the street to help with expenses without the knowledge of my parents, who wouldn't let him work. My father's dream had been that he should only spend his spare time in study, so at least one of his sons would get somewhere in life and break the cycle of poverty. The thing is, the teacher hadn't told them ether would cause death if it were held to a person's nose for more than a few seconds. It all could have been avoided. When my brother returned home early the next morning, happy because of the money he had brought for our parents, he removed the rags from their faces to find them all cold and dead."

The stranger lit a cigarette. He took a long drag and continued, "The second I heard this, I slashed at my wrist with that same razor and killed myself. I died. I lay in the morgue for a night. But the next morning, one of the guards saw that condensation had formed on the plastic that covered my face. When I was taken to the clinic, they saw I was still alive, even though my artery was completely severed and black."

The sad stranger breathed out, then sucked forcefully on the cigarette, showing his left wrist to the villager. There was a deep wound underneath a leather wristband; it was clear that the vein had been torn down the middle and was still black. The villager, still sharpening his knife slowly, glanced down at the man's arm. The sad man asked, "You're sure you still want to hear more?" The villager answered, "Of course, if you promise to listen to my story afterwards."

Putting the cigarette to his lips, the sad man looked at the villager's hands as they slowly, calmly, sharpened the knife. He stared at the unhurried movement of the knife on the rock, and continued, "They brought me up to the gallows three more times; but each time the rope snapped. After that, they threw me out of prison, hush hush, because they believed I was so cursed that I didn't even deserve to die. I was determined to kill the teacher who had left that lesson so incomplete, but that very night I was sleeping on the side of the road and for the very first time had a dream about my mother. She was living in a glass house without any openings. I was walking around a glass room feeling as if it might crack and shatter at any moment. There was nothing in the house. My mother was standing by a wall looking outside. When she saw me, she touched my hair tenderly and said, 'If I had known you were still alive, I would have visited you, every week.' Then she handed me a sack. She caressed my hands and pointing, said, 'Take this sack and go that way.' When I woke up, I found this bag on the ground beside me. It's full of letters prisoners have written to their families. Since that day, I have been travelling in the direction my mother indicated, and on the way, I deliver the messages, knowing that if mothers know their children are alive in prison, they will visit them."

The stranger took a drag on his cigarette, then stamped it out and said, "But I still haven't figured out why she wanted me to come this way . . . north."

"Once you understand, you will die," said the villager, coolly. For a second the sad man's eyes flashed. He paused and said, "I've been dead from the very first time I stood at the gallows, but nobody knows it." The villager said, "Then listen to this," and picked at his tooth with his sharp knife. "My family was also very poor. Years before I was born, my father travelled through forests and mountains, from village to village and from city to city, until he reached Tehran. There, after years of hardship and labor, he managed to build a small brick kiln with his own two hands. But several months later, he was killed. One evening before he died, my father dreamed that a snake came out of his sleeve and bit him. The very next day he told my mother that he owed his apprentice one hundred tomans, and money also to several other people; so, he instructed her what to do were he to die. Right then and there, my mother removed her wedding ring, rolled up the carpet from under their feet and told him to sell them, pay back his debts and give some alms to ward off death. However, after my father sold the items he spent some on a burial shroud and a few things for a funeral. He put one hundred tomans in his pocket to give to his apprentice and the rest he put in my mother's cupboard. At noon that day before my father had a chance to pay him, his angry apprentice stabbed him to death. When my mother heard what had happened, she languished and died of sorrow leaving me, just ten years old at the time, to begin begging and working as a laborer, passing from city to city and village to village, until I arrived here. The first night I was here I dreamed of my father. He was living in a windowless glass house without any furniture that I was afraid would shatter and fall in on him at any moment. He caressed and kissed my feet tenderly and said, 'If I had known how much you would suffer I would have given the alms.' Then he moved towards one of the glass walls and pointed to the square beyond and said, 'Go and wait at that square with a knife.'" The villager showed the sad man his knife and said, "This is the same knife that killed my father." At this, the sad-eyed stranger stood up and said, "Before I die, allow me to kiss your hand."

The villager stretched his hand out coolly toward the stranger. The sad man kissed it and said, "I am grateful to you for helping me attain what I desire." In silence, they slowly walked together to the depths of the forest and, once far out of sight from the village, the villager plunged the knife down to the hilt into the sad man's heart. With mournful eyes the villager would never forget, and smiling faintly, the sad man died. Afterwards, as the villager was about to throw the body and knife into a swamp to feed the maggots and insects, he looked into the dead man's eyes for the first time and gave a start. Seeing the dilated pupils, he realized that the man was nothing like the person he had spent a lifetime waiting for, hating. The villager stared at those pupils until nightfall. Then he lit a small

fire and spent a week looking through its flames at the body
that was slowly swelling and beginning to stink, preyed upon
by maggots and cockroaches and snakes. And so it continued,
until his nose became as filled with putrid stench as his life had
been with loathing. Eventually, he was so repulsed by the
birthing maggots and snake and scorpion infestations, that he
despised himself. When the stench of the corpse became so
foul that nearby flowers wilted and butterflies and dragonflies
diverted from their course, he dumped the knife and what was
left of the body into the swamp. Then he slung the man's heavy
backpack over his shoulder and set off towards distant villages.
But first, reaching the top of our hill and Dad, who was sitting
on the porch, he gave the news in a clear, quiet voice and left.

Dad was relieved to have news of Sohrab at last, momentar-
ily thinking, *What sad eyes that man has*. After coming into the
house to collect his things, he set off for Tehran immediately.
He didn't know, nor would he find out later that, before being
transferred to Evin prison, Sohrab had spent eleven days in the
nearest city—left forgotten, in a solitary confinement cell.

Dad never knew that after the Revolutionary Guard shoved
Sohrab into the cell, he went to the locker-room, changed his
clothes, signed a leave paper, and left: to spend eleven days in
his village near Ardabil to celebrate his wedding, sleep with his
wife, and get her pregnant before coming back. Upon his
return, while drinking tea and chatting with his colleagues, he
asked what had happened to the boy from Tehran. It was then
that everyone asked, "Who!?" and rushed towards the solitary
confinement cell at the end of the long, dank, dark underground corridor where Sohrab, contorted in delusion and terror, hunger and death, was taking his last breaths. Eleven days
before, when that soldier had departed, leaving him without
food or water, at first Sohrab thought somebody would come
to interrogate him a few hours later. From the very beginning,
the stench in the cell had given him a headache: the smell of

urine mixed with fresh blood, puss, sweat and vomit. He tried to comfort himself by thinking someone would soon come and tell him what lay in store. It was pitch black. He stood up and tried to get a sense of the size of the cell. One step wide, three steps long. About the size of his grave. There wasn't even the smallest opening, or at least not one that could be made out in the thick darkness. He put his ear to the iron door and heard a faint sound in the distance. After several hours without the slightest sound coming from outside, the first wave of fear welled up inside him. The fear of being forgotten. Terrified, he got up and began banging on the door, then kicking it, frantically. After several more hours of struggle, frightened, hungry and thirsty, he groped blindly along the wall and found an extremely short tap near the floor, but it was so low to the ground his cheek was pressed against the floor as he drank, greedily; the taste of rust filling his mouth. He didn't know if it was the water or his anxiety that was making his stomach churn. There was no toilet. Another hour passed. In the end, he had no choice, however, but to relieve himself right there and wash himself with the same tap. The smell of fear-induced diarrhea made him throw up several times. He removed his clothes and threw them over his excrement to mask the smell—to no avail.

The delusions began. Fear. Feeling close to death. Suffocation. Vomit. To comfort himself, he wanted to draw parallels between himself and all the protagonists in the political novels he had read, but their names had vanished from memory. He couldn't even remember the music he liked and usually listened to, on the stereo. From those very first hours he couldn't distinguish day from night.

By the third day, he could no longer recall the day of the month; and by the seventh he couldn't even remember what day, of what month, of what year it was. He had stared so long into the blackness in front of him, into the vacuum, into the

eyes of death, his eyes were bulging from their sockets, and it felt
as if the capillaries in his eyeballs had run dry. His saliva had
dried, making him cough again and again. He put his hands on
the wall and traced scratches that had been made with a finger-
nail or a sharp object, trying to guess what letters had been
hacked there. Once he managed to read a complete sentence:
*The third world is a place where we share the same pain but not
the same path.* No matter how hard he thought, he couldn't
remember who that quote was from. He removed his belt from
his pants. If he didn't keep himself occupied, he would go crazy.
He wanted to scratch a poem into the wall with the prong of his
belt buckle but he quickly forgot what he wanted to write. He
was so hungry he stuffed fallen plaster into his mouth. His dry
tongue burned and he began coughing even more. From the
seventh day onward, he couldn't even muster the energy to drag
himself to the door to press his ear against straining to hear distant sounds that, recently, had sounded like people whispering
a plot to murder him. The indistinct voices were conspiring on
how they would come to strangle him in the dark. The voices
blended together. The laugh and howl of a murderer, torturer,
interrogator; and the person whose job it was to pull the stool
out from beneath the condemned at the gallows. On the eighth
day, no matter how long he groped along the floor, he couldn't
even find a cockroach to eat, like the character in a book whose
title he couldn't recall. Then he even thought of eating his own
excrement to stay alive and prove to those filthy animals who
had thrown him away like a dog that he could survive in spite
of them. He picked up a piece of dried poop with his shirt and
tried to convince himself it probably tasted like mud. But
before he could even lift it to his mouth, he vomited so violently
he spewed all that was left of the bitter bile in his gut over the
wall. After that, he couldn't remember anything. Not fear. Not
scary delusional voices. Not hunger. Not death. Not sorrow.
Not missing Mom, Dad, Beeta, or me.

*

He didn't know how much time had gone by when he saw a little sliver of light through the crack in his eyes. He found himself lying in a bed with IVs connected to both arms; and heard a slap, pummeling punches and kicks, and then someone yelling, "If he'd died, whod'a been held responsible then, you jackass, Azeri!?" The next day, the nurse changing his IV whispered in his ear that the Revolutionary Guard who'd left him for dead only received a mere month of additional military duty. Everything was over. It seemed as if nothing had happened. As if he wasn't meant to stay alive. Or perhaps the plan was to bring him back from the brink of death, to then execute him in a ceremony befitting of the Revolution.

Three weeks later, when Sohrab was handed over to the provincial prison and Dad went there to inquire about him, he was given the same answer he'd heard before, "Who?" The soldier looked at the list, shook his head, and said empathetically, "No sir, we don't have anyone by that name."

As Dad went from city to city looking for his son and our brother, they moved Sohrab like a hot potato from city to city, beating him so severely he peed blood and one of his kidneys failed. Finally, they decided to transfer him to Tehran so that his blood wouldn't be on their hands. His one-page file in which he had been accused of evading military duty and reading various Fedai Guerrilla pamphlets, swelled to justify the move. It was thus that with a broken jaw, crushed rib and only one functioning kidney, Sohrab was sent to Tehran, where Mom, Dad, and Beeta were able to see him for the first time in five months. And throughout the visit, they all joked and laughed—so much so that other visitors glared at them, annoyed.

Mom despised herself that day—eight years after we had come to Razan—because she had no choice but to don a headscarf for the first time. Eight years before, when we decided to leave Tehran for this remote village, she had vowed not to leave the village or even the grove as long as the regime was in power just so she wouldn't have to put one on. For eight years, she kept herself busy with books, chickens, roosters, rain, music, and memories; and even when news came of the death of a relative in the flooding in Darband on July 26, 1987, she didn't leave the grove so as not to be forced to wear a headscarf for the funeral. Neither could she be contented to put one on to go to Tehran in an act of solidarity with a child and his family when she heard that one thirteen-year-old relative had been sentenced to seventy lashes in Enghelab Square[2] just for eating a greengage plum during Ramadan. She said she didn't want to witness mass violence. Mom would say, "Once your eyes get accustomed to seeing violence in city streets and squares, they can only become more accustomed. Gradually you'll turn into your enemy; the very person who spread the violence." Mom wasn't surprised when she learned years later that the thirteen-year-old child, harboring hate for the Iranian people, had left for France, never to look back. She didn't blame him because she had heard that on the day, the man charged with carrying out the punishment had taken pity on the skinny, thirteen-year-old boy and tried to hit his back lightly. But the people gathered in the street watching the scene, greedily, as though it were some sort of street performance, yelled, "You're hitting too lightly! . . . Again! . . . Start again! . . . From the beginning!" And so, instead of seventy lashes, he received ninety-three. Later, the boy told his family that pressing himself against the ground in pain as the sharp blows hit his skin and delicate bones, he promised himself that if he made it out alive, he would take whichever opportunity came first: revenge on the people or flight from them, forever. Several years later, he

[2] Literally, Revolution Square.

fled over the Turkish border to Europe, and we heard that he had changed his name and identity— anytime he was asked where he came from he would say, "Greece!"

Despite this, Mom didn't know *the inevitable is inevitable,* as Dad would say, and that one day she would have to break her own rule to visit her dear son. It was thus that when they went to meet Sohrab after five months of silence and found him twenty kilos lighter, not only did they pretend not to notice, but they laughed and talked to alleviate the pressure inflicted both by Mom's mandatory hijab and Sohrab's arbitrary imprisonment. Mom asked how the food was and Sohrab, with a laugh, said it was great. Dad asked if he knew when he'd be released. Laughing again, Sohrab said it was news to him that they would release him at all! Then to change the subject, Beeta said they had looked for Bahar everywhere so she could come and visit him, too, but they hadn't been able to find her. She was neither in the chicken coop nor the stable! Sohrab laughed and said he wasn't worried because he had had a dream about me the night before. Dad asked very earnestly, "So, how was Bahar? What did she say?" Everyone laughed, but Sohrab said very earnestly that I had told him, *life goes on.* And so it was that the thirty-minute visit was spent joking. Everyone was happy that Sohrab had only been arrested by mistake and would soon be released. However, when Mom accidentally overheard other visitors, all similarly lighthearted, she began to feel uneasy. But by then it untimely was too late to show any concern because the prison guard's bell rang out, making everyone jump.

There was a ruckus in the big prison yard, filling some unwitting visitors with the fleeting hope that protests to bring down the Islamic regime had finally begun. In those days, many people were so naive that the slightest commotion, gun shot, sudden blackout of a television program, electricity, or anything else unusual, prompted joyous shouts of, "They've come . . . They've come!" But who had come? Nobody knew. So, when the first swallow flew into the small window, high on the wall of the visiting room, the guard panicked and sent a shower of bullets towards the glass because he, too, had instantly thought, *They've come . . . They've come.*

Everyone held their breath as they watched the bloody swallow with shredded feathers fall to the ground and take its last breath. The guard, the prisoners, and the visitors were still aghast at the unexpected shots when a second swallow flew in through the broken window. Then another, and another. In the blink of an eye, the room was filled with chortling birds whose song struck anxiety into hearts. Unaware of what he was doing, Dad cried, "The swallows . . . the swallows!" Officers fired at the frightened, confused birds. Suddenly the air was black and the sound of shots ricocheted off the surfaces. Terrified, people covered their heads with their hands and were herded out into the yard at the end of gun barrels, without saying goodbye to their detained, loved ones. The yard was drowning in bullets, feathers, and the corpses of thousands of swallows who had mistaken several days of spring-like weather for migration season, and so had taken to the skies over Tehran. In the large rectangular yard the terrified, disoriented swallows flew into people, prison walls and barbed wire as they were shot at by officers. Dead birds rained down like black hail. Several people were shot. Bloody human and swallow bodies fell to the ground in the prison yard at Evin; and people, still being driven out the back door, trampled them, screamed, and shed tears for them. An old man, weeping and yelling, "The poor swallows . . . the poor swallows!" was hit in the mouth with the butt of a gun.

Just thirty minutes later, the sky was once again clear and blue, indifferent to the blackness of migrating birds just minutes before the prison yard was littered with swallow feathers and the blood-stained corpses of birds and visitors killed by mistake. Officers were sitting at the edges of the yard, resting and looking at the bloody bird corpses whose black and white feathers were still suspended in midair. Who would have thought all those forlorn birds would be killed just because they miscalculated the season? One of the officers laughed at this thought. Then another and another. The high prison walls bounced the armed officers' guffaws from one wall to the next. A wind blew into the Evin prison yard, over the heights of Northern Tehran, over the victorious guffawing officers, taking the floating feathers over Evin's tall walls to fall one by one on houses and oblivious people as they rushed over endless distances from one end of the city to another just as on any other day. Back and forth. Back and forth. An hour later, one of the bloody, bullet-riddled swallow feathers stuck to the windshield of a silver Buick Skylight whose driver, teary-eyed and terrified, was driving northwards in silence. Towards the forest. To the least likely place to ever see another human being, again.

CHAPTER 4

A t exactly the same time the swallows were being massacred in the skies above Evin, Mom, Dad, and Beeta were running to and fro under a spray of bullets; Sohrab was looking miserably at the bloody swallows from the one little window in his cell; and I was wandering freely down the house's winding corridors, peeking into all the rooms, and occasionally pilfering something. I go into Dad's workroom located behind the kitchen with a small door connecting it to the backyard. The room is filled with wood, books and tools for carpentry and framing. Then, just as Ms. Henna, Mom's favorite chicken, enters the room to take advantage of the empty house to leave her turds anywhere she wants and snoop around just as I have, I find the photo I've spent months searching for. It is in a yellow envelope next to Dad's other photos: Dad with this favorite *tar*; Dad making a *tar*; Dad beside Jalil Shahnaz, Farhang Sharif, Pirniakan[3]; Dad with his arms wrapped around me from behind, as we play *tar* together. This is the photo I've been after. I take it and slip it under my dress to join several walnuts left over from that morning. In the corner of Dad's workroom is an old dust-covered love seat and a table with everything on it. Everything but a *tar*. Everything from an ashtray to a reading lamp, and an old aquarium without any fish or water, but filled with shells; shells that Dad

[3] Famous Iranian *tar* masters who have playing styles named after them.

collects from the seashore. Dad's had this mania for shells for a while now. It started at the same time that Mom got her mania for fireflies; she would go into the forest every night, returning with jars full of them. When everyone was asleep, Mom would release the fireflies she had caught on the edge of the forest and let them fly around. Unaware that I was always watching her, she would lie down in the middle of the floor and look at them; at fireflies that shone like stars and made love in the layers of her hair. One night when Mom came to share her anguished insomnia, induced by Sohrab's arrest, with the fireflies, the house's silence and the shadows, she found me surrounded by them, and shining. I giggled, and she looked at me horrified, her hair disheveled. That night Mom sat down next to me on the floor and allowed us to share the harmony of the fireflies. That was the night I realized how little I still knew her, my mother, the woman alongside whom I eat three meals a day, who tucks me in every night and whose gentle *Goodnight* is the last safe sound to echo through the house. That night, she shared one of her poems with me. It was from her life before marriage; a time she had dreamed of becoming a poet. Keeping her eyes closed and leaning against the low table, surrounded by twinkling fireflies, she recited:

The Creator with himself always content
Surrounded by hope and joy, fireflies, one day is alone.
The end of the world.
With no nightly disturbance, a cry:
O Creator, where is your justice?

During those sleepless nights, Dad would peek into Beeta's and my room, worrying about Sohrab's fate, and then drive his silver Buick Skylight to the coast. He would sit on the damp sand and listen to the frightening sound of waves at night. He would examine shells with a torch and fill his pockets with a colorful collection, returning home and rearranging them in the empty aquarium, until morning. Sometimes Dad still wakes up in the middle of the night and tunes into American radio to listen to political news inside Iran. Radio is the only form of mass communication in our home. Whenever the presenter on *Voice of America* announces, between news stories, music by Iranian singers who fled Iran to America after the Revolution, he turns down the volume and presses one of the large shells to his ear to listen to the sea. He closes his eyes and inhales deeply on his pipe, stretching his legs out on the couch, just like in the old days when we would all go to Hotel Ghou; like those times when there were no Revolutionary Guards to call us bourgeois, or accuse Beeta of acts against national security because her headscarf was pushed too far back on her head. And sometimes, while sawing a piece of wood, applying finish or preparing marbled paper for his calligraphy, Dad listens to his favorite singers. He listens to Delkash, who now lives who knows where, or Marzieh or Vigan; to Haideh who fled to America after the Revolution:

For my sad house
for my sad alley
for you, for all those like us
it is singing I'm sad.

Or Banan, singing:

Every night like a flute I moan in sorrow
You took my heart and soul but did not become my lover
You were with me, you left without me
Like the fragrance of a flower where have you gone?
Alone I am left, alone you have gone.

Sometimes in the middle of the night, Mom would wake

up, too, and they would cut wood or apply finish together. One night when the political news anchor for *Voice of America* broke the silence between them, they didn't even look at each other, because in their mind's eye each was looking at Sohrab. They just sawed wood: *rr-rr, rr-rr, rr-rr*. The anchor was saying, now that Ayatollah Khomeini had agreed to end the eight-year war and the Security Council Resolution 598 had been signed, there were signs that he would avenge this defeat; so dark things lay in store for Iran, but no political analyst could predict yet what this might be. Dad thought Mom was crying while Mom thought it was Dad.

Early in the morning when, to the sound of my favorite rooster, Captain Namu, Mom and Dad came to, they saw that dawn was breaking and found the floor littered with misshapen pieces of cut wood they didn't know what to do with. At first Dad reprimanded Mom for ruining all their frame wood. Then Mom yelled at Dad for putting all the wood in front of her. In the end, they both started laughing; and they laughed so hard tears rolled down their cheeks. Then Dad took Mom's head in his arms so her sobs and wailing wouldn't disturb our early morning slumber.

The place that most resembled our ancestral home was under the rafters. It was full of mice that scurried up and down satin cloth, tables of inlaid wood, and portraits of ancestors living and dead, that even ate the mothballs. It was a place full of stashes of notebooks and paper and termite-infested handwritten books and old photographs; full of fine old carpets, *jajims*, and *kelims* that Mom had stashed so the mice, moths, and termites would annihilate as much of them as quickly as possible. Mom so detested life after the Revolution that she was afraid to look at the past, fearing that even the smallest object would remind her of past happiness. That's why there were mice everywhere. Sometimes, when the sound of mice and termites under the rafters got really loud, Mom would go up and sit on one of the dusty couches in the steamy, suffocating air and look at the mice's feast; the beauty and history gnawed away bit by bit. All of those things made up decades of memories and past identity. They had survived for centuries. *We are not the first people to have destroyed ourselves; with a city where all devices of happiness were present*, she thought. Then she would descend teary-eyed and get as far away from the house as possible. She would sit under a tree in the forest and sob. Once she had cried herself out, she would come back, her nose red, eyes puffy, and begin cooking, slowly humming a poem by Shamlou in her beautiful voice:

Slept the sun and the earth slept
like a mother at the death of her son, wept.
Turned to the dark tent of night, haggard,
the sea to the death of my happiness, laggard.

It was an unspoken agreement that we all accepted, and indeed honored unconcerned, Mom's strange love for Sohrab. Sohrab wasn't just Mom's darling twenty-six-year-old son. For Mom, Sohrab wasn't a son awaiting an uncertain fate, imprisoned in an uncertain prison. For Mom, he was the culmination of heartbeats, desires, loves and hopes that she had endured her entire life; of which she dreamed, for which she searched in novels and in the layers of poetry; and which in the end, she lost. She never said a word when Sohrab was arrested, yet she was certain of his fate. She was the only one who knew, with the possible exception of me. She who, although seconds earlier had been going over her dream from the night before, attained enlightenment atop the greengage tree the very moment Sohrab was executed. The night before Sohrab's execution, Mom had woken terrified from a dream and, clutching at her left breast, she thought, *they've killed Sohrab.* Then, looking anxiously at a spot of blood on her shirt, she lifted it and on her left breast saw the marks of two tiny baby teeth that had drawn blood exactly where Sohrab had done, when he was a baby. It was right after seeing that drop of blood that an invisible force pulled her up the greengage tree, to be stricken by that silent mania, that sudden enlightenment.

Long before we learned of the connection between Sohrab's name and Mom's teenage love, we had heard that when she was pregnant with him she had dreamed that while in her stomach he had dreamed he was crawling naked in a dense forest. He crawls and crawls before stopping in front of a tree just like other trees, and crawls up it. After a short while, he pauses before continuing. Now the baby realizes that when he moves, the tree grows and when he stops, it stops. The baby continues to climb higher and higher and the tree grows taller and taller. He climbs so high, and the tree grows so tall and broad, that it consumes half of the earth. When the baby reaches the top of the huge tree, he looks at the ground below, pauses, is absorbed into the bark, and disappears.

Later, when she described the dream at Sohrab's fifteenth birthday party, everyone offered an interpretation. Except Sohrab. He just shrugged his shoulders and with his usual humor said, "Well, I for one, don't remember anything."

When Sohrab was still around, one of our summer pastimes was to use badminton rackets to catch baby mice in the rooms and rafters. Then the three of us siblings would hold a field trial to decide their fate, and issue and execute the final ruling before Dad—the murderer of mice—got home. "The death of a baby mouse won't fix anything. The laws of nature should not be violated. It would be better not to have blood on our hands." The three of us would mercifully release the terrified mice from the corner of the attic and, satisfied and smiling, would watch them disappear into the distance. But now it is a precious treasure trove of Iranian handicrafts that has fallen prey to the mice under the rafters. And yet compared to what's in Granddad's house, it wouldn't even fill up a small trunk of antiques. In the autumn of 1961 when Mom first saw Dad's house and family, the magnificence of that big, eighteen-bedroom house with its corridors and vestibules, dais and terrace left her speechless and, for a moment, unable to move. If Dad hadn't put his arm around her and guided her forward in time, she surely would have shamed herself in front of her husband's mother Gordafarid, and his father Jamshid, as the first daughter-in-law of the family. In fact, the house was a Qajar mansion whose halls, vestibules, and corridors with their gilding, plasterwork and mirrors drew stares and took the breath of anyone who first entered it. It was full of objects that Roza had only read about in books and whose pictures she had seen in magazines: colorful Iranian, Chinese, and Indian silks, valanced chairs, velvet Iranian drapes, hundred-armed crystal chandeliers, porcelain vases and violet tulips, porcelain dishes decorated with flowers and birds, paisley-covered cushions; rare silk carpets from Nain and Kashan; portraits of Qajar and Pahlavi Shahs and Zakariya Razi, the family's great ancestor; inlaid and carved tables and chairs from Isfahani masters, Italian furniture, silver dishes; and a bookcase with books in every language from Russian, Chinese, English, French and German, to Tibetan, Sanskrit, Aramaic, Pahlavi, Latin and Arabic. With its books and both traditional and modern furnishings, the house was a combination of the Qajar and Pahlavi eras. Just like its inhabitants. That day in particular Dad, who was just twenty-five, had been on his way back from a week in a small cave he had found near Abshar Dogholu. During that week, he had played his *tar* until blood dripped from his fingertips and red lichen had sprouted from the stones and blossomed. On his way back, it was not yet dark on the slopes of Darband when his eye alighted on Mom who, so engrossed in a collection of poetry by Sohrab Sepehri, saw neither the people around her nor the beautiful orange sunset. This allowed Dad to observe her for a long time. Mom didn't raise her head until she had finished reading *The Wayfarer*. When she did raise her eyes, she was no longer in this world and saw no one. She was travelling in a universe in which she and Sohrab were the only voyagers. From her surroundings, she heard nothing but buzzing. Just one phrase echoed in her mind like the sound of repeated thunder on the windows of a lone bedroom at night:

And love, only love
carried me to the expanse of life's sorrow
delivered me to the places to become a bird.

Dad approached Mom right then and there, and had he not used his intelligence, he would have lost her, forever. He was clever enough to begin the conversation with a poem by Sepehri and provide Mom with new information on the poet, so that from the very first moment, she felt they had much to talk about. It was thus that at not yet ten o'clock at night, Roza did the most daring thing she had ever done in her life: she agreed to marry the man who would become my father, without the counsel or permission of her only family—her mother. A mullah, cold and fearful of dark specters and fog, appeared out of the darkness on the slope and agreed to marry them right then and there, for twenty tomans.

It was only years later when Beeta, Sohrab, and I asked Mom and Dad why Sohrab's name, unlike ours, started with the letter 'S,' that Mom finally told the story of how she had gone to buy books on Naser Khosrow Street, which at the time was where all the bookshops were, and had bought *The Wayfarer*, which had just been published. While reading that long poem, her feet had suddenly been lifted from the ground and she flew above passersby and booksellers as misty rain fell on her *Wayfarer*. Puffing on his pipe, Dad listened intently as Mom recalled that day. Reading *The Wayfarer* under the gentle rain, then noticing with surprise that her feet had detached from the earth and that she was flying over people in Naser Khosrow Street, it was the hand of a young man on her shoulder that brought her back. He was extremely thin and his thick beard made him look like a hippie. Had it not been for his kind and polite words, Mom would have reacted harshly to this skinny, little bearded man who brought her feet back firmly to the cobblestones of Naser Khosrow Street. He looked at Mom and told her she'd dropped her wallet. Without thanking him she retrieved it and, still engrossed—*My heart is singularly sad and nothing/ not the fragrant moments falling silent on the branches of the bitter orange/ nor the honest words in the silence between two matthiola petals/ no, nothing from the empty throng all around/ can free me*—she continued on her way. However, she had taken no more than a few steps before the same young man again placed his hand on Mom's shoulder, only this time to ask her if she would be willing to join him for a coffee. Mom's favorable reaction surprised both of them so much that they laughed. Two hours later, after having discussed the living flowing spirit in *The Wayfarer's* verses; and Roza—who had just finished high school—having spoken of her dream of becoming a poet; and the young man had told of his mysterious journey to India from which he had just returned; and they had both shared so much of themselves that their coffee had become cold twice, Roza suddenly remembered that she had to get home as soon as possible lest her old, solitary mother become anxious. It wasn't until their hurried goodbye, when premature darkness made Roza run from him into the streaming rain to cross the crowded Shah Reza Street, that she heard his name through the din of car horns, violent acceleration and squeal of brakes: Sohrab Sepehri.

Mom says that when she heard his name, her knees went weak and she was almost run over by a car. She wanted to run back across the street. She wanted to scream. She wanted to call out to him. She wanted to say to him, "Don't go . . . Stay . . ." But it was too late. Sohrab had disappeared in the throng of people running in the sudden rain, while Roza was left standing there with the noise of horns and braking all around, a Parker pen the young man had given her as a memento, in her hand. This was the very pen that years later would be capriciously stolen from on top of her desk by a mullah who had come with several Revolutionary Guards to arrest her son, several months later, Sohrab. Perhaps it was fear of loss that prompted her to accept my father, Hushang's marriage proposal. She mustn't lose another Sohrab. Later, when Mom admitted to Dad that if she had seen Sohrab Sepehri just one more time she would never have let him go, Dad wasn't too upset because from his many literary and musical circles he heard from friends that Sohrab was an otherworldly poet who had never had a girlfriend and didn't want to marry. This turned out to be correct. Years and years later, on April 21, 1980 when newspapers ran the headline: AUTHOR OF *THE WAYFARER* DEPARTS ON ETERNAL VOYAGE, Sohrab was still single. Dad let her find the news out for herself rather than breaking her heart any earlier than necessary. Several months later, when Roza was flipping through Dad's journals and read about Sohrab Sepehri's death, Hushang left her alone for the whole day to cry for her departed wayfarer.

Walking around the attic among deserted holy objects, I remember it is also the place of pleasure and merrymaking for the ghosts of the family's deceased. That is what Beeta says. She who believes that on many occasions she heard footsteps, snickering and the click of the light switch being turned on and off, coming from under the rafters. Beeta says that however resistant the people in this family might be to death, the clan's dead are not few in number. Once, when Beeta was sitting in Dad's workroom to take advantage of its coolness and read a book in Dad's absence, she saw a rickety old man with a white silk cloak and white Zoroastrian hat descend the steps from the attic. Looking at him wide-eyed, Beeta recognized him immediately and said, "You've come all this way to frighten me?" He was none other than our ancestor, Zakariya Razi, the tenth-century scholar, discoverer of alcohol and author of one hundred and eighty-four books on medicine, alchemy and philosophy; who was excommunicated by other newly converted Muslim Iranians for writing two books on the uselessness and fraudulence of the prophets, which were then burned. When our great ancestor came down the steps with hunched back and eyes weakened from mercury gas and steam, he turned to Beeta and said, "There is something you need to do." Frightened, Beeta asked, "Why me?" The frail old man answered, "Because you will be the trunk's sole heir." "What trunk?" Beeta asked. The great ancestor said, "You'll understand later. You have to promise to protect the trunk from their evil until the appointed time." He moved his eyes and eyebrows in such a way as he said 'their' that Beeta understood who he meant.

To be rid of him sooner, Beeta said, "Alright, I promise. But how will I know what to do? The people you're afraid of are everywhere. Even here." The old man sat on the last step and said thoughtfully, "You're right."

Then both of them sunk into thought. As Beeta looked at the pale wrinkled skin on the old man's hands and face, her fear slowly melted away and was replaced with pity. She really wanted to do something for him. That's why she said, "As soon as you can send me somewhere where I will be free of *them*, I will do as promised." The old man thought for a moment and said, "Where, for example?" Beeta said, "I don't know, either. You think about it."

Upon hearing this, the old man got up and, just as he had descended the stairs with measured steps, he ascended them in a dignified and deliberate manner until he merged with the dirt and grime on the carpets and reams of Qajar-era cloth collecting dust under the rafters. After the old man left, Beeta forgot all about the encounter until years later when her hand brushed against her slimy fish tail and this conversation, long submerged in murky oblivion, resurfaced once again.

Up until then, I had only seen a wandering ghost once. One rainy night when I was sleeping in my treehouse, I was awoken by a cool, wet smell. It was obvious someone was there—there was no need to turn on a light. Whoever it was approached slowly, pulled up the wick on lantern and lit a match. It was the wandering ghost of a Siberian hunter who had lost his way many years ago. I got up and handed him a cup of water and two baked potatoes because I knew that wandering ghosts were always hungry and thirsty. Without saying a word, he sat down in the corner and ate voraciously. As he was eating he asked me for salt, which I gave to him. After drinking the water, he asked for more. Then, although I had asked for nothing, he showed me his deer hide clothes from which a few pieces of rabbit and fox skin and several large handmade hunting knives were hanging. He said he was a Siberian hunter and that when he was alive, he had been fooled by a shaman who had told him if he could kill a big bear he would help him marry the chief's daughter whom he loved. However, the large bear ripped him apart and ate him, after which the shaman married the chief's daughter, instead. The old man said he was only twenty years old when he died, but he learned later that even dead people age gradually. Since his death, he had been consumed with a desire for vengeance. Even after one thousand years, however, he had not yet had the opportunity for revenge, although he had managed to behead the shaman in four different lives and stab him once—but this wasn't enough. In his last life, the shaman had finally used some of the shamanic tricks he remembered from previous lives and had trapped the hunter's ghost in a tornado. After three days and nights of spinning and twirling in the tornado's eye, the hunter landed, but now, centuries later, he was still unable to find his way back to Siberia. In the spiritual realm, he was of an entirely different rank from the ghosts who could be found in this region, so his questions couldn't be answered easily by the ignorant specters who didn't even know where Siberia was or where in the world they themselves were. I assured him that I knew where it was and that I knew it was towards the north, but that if he wanted a proper address he should return the following night so that I could show him on a map. The old man, hardly believing I could save him from his several-hundred-year-long peregrination, evaporated into the air, reciting Siberian spells.

The next night, I brought a map of the world and, sitting with the old man in the light of the lantern, I showed him where we were and where he had to go. Throughout my explanation, he asked questions and touched the various colors on the map that indicated separate countries. Then he fell silent. It was a long silence. At first I thought the old man's silence was one of satisfaction, but slowly I realized he had fallen into a philosophical stupor. When he finally opened his mouth, not taking his eyes from the map, he said, "So, the thing on which I lived is called Planet Earth, and it's round, and according to you, all of these countries and tribal lands exist, and seven billion people live on this ball, and I don't even know how many that is. I just know it means very many."

Then he paused and said, "It means very, very, very many. Many more than all the Siberian tribes." I had bent over the map and was waiting to see what his conclusion would be. After much contemplation, he said, "It doesn't seem to be worth it anymore." I was happy to hear those familiar words. I was just about to ask him what he was going to do when he said, "Well, if there are all these people alive, think of all the dead people and wandering ghosts who also live on this ball. If every one of these wandering ghosts wanted to avenge themselves on another ghost or person, the world would become hell." Then he looked at me with his dark, almond-shaped eyes, filled his sunburnt, unsmiling lips with air, and finally let out a laugh. His laugh made me laugh. His laugh gradually got louder and louder until it gave fright to sleepy birds, and here and there lights came on in nearby houses. Then the Siberian hunter got up and, laughing deliriously, walked out the door and disappeared into the air waving to me from behind. He held his other hand over his belly, still shaking with laughter.

At the end of that long, ill-fated day when all the errant swallows were executed in the skies over Evin, I finished my rounds among the memories that dwell in the house and attic. At that precise time, Mom, Dad, and Beeta were being held up by a bunch of Basijis[4] and Revolutionary Guards who had improvised a traffic stop and were pulling over cars on the road to Firuzkuh, to inspect bags and boots for any forbidden objects. There was neither alcohol nor music cassettes in Dad's car, nor recordings of speeches by Massoud Rajavi[5] or Kianouri[6]; there were no speeches by Khomeini at the Feyzieh Madrasa in

[4] Basijis: young volunteer members of the Basij, an auxiliary force set up after the Revolution that is engaged in activities such as internal security, law enforcement, organizing public religious ceremonies, policing morals, and suppression of dissident gatherings.

[5] Leader of the People's Mojahedin.

[6] 1915–1999. Leader of the Tudeh Party.

Qom[7]; there was not even backgammon or a deck of cards. There was perhaps just a book forgotten in one of its recesses. From the moment a fourteen-year-old Basiji with a G3 assault rifle over his shoulder approached their car, kicked a tire, and, without even looking at Dad, said jeeringly, "It's a foreign car!" to when they were finally given permission to get back in and leave, Mom, Dad, and Beeta had stood on the side of the road shivering in the cold for two and a half hours. Their car was turned inside out and, finally, when the Guards found *One Hundred Years of Solitude* by García Márquez in Beeta's bag, they spent an hour passing it back and forth and radioing around before they were eventually convinced that politically, it was not a dangerous book. When Dad's car began to move off at last, seeing that he had had no excuse to show off in front of Beeta, who was a pretty girl, the Basiji boy spat the shells of his sunflower seeds onto Beeta's window and smiled, revealing rotten teeth.

[7] One of Khomeini's first speeches in 1963, in which he admonished the Shah but at the same time said he didn't want the Shah to be overthrown nor the people to be happy about his departure.

CHAPTER 5

Thickness here are a lot of good things about dying. You are suddenly light and free and no longer afraid of death, sickness, judgement or religion; you don't have to grow up fated to replicate the lives of others. You are no longer forced to study nor tested on the principles of religion or what invalidates prayer. But for me the most important advantage of death is knowing something when I want to know it. *Kon fayakon*.[8] Piece of cake. If I want to be somewhere, I am, just like that. I realized all this the day I died. February 9, 1979. Just two days before the culmination of the Islamic Revolution. I died the day inflamed revolutionaries boiling with revolutionary hatred and fervor poured into our house in Tehranpars and, making strange noises, cried out, "God is great, God is great!" They stormed Dad's basement workshop and, after pouring kerosene on all his handmade *tars*, the mulberry wood with which he crafted them, and his books, set everything alight. I was just thirteen years old and was down there practicing *tar*. When they savagely attacked, I crawled under the table, paralyzed by fear. I saw with my own eyes how they splashed petrol everywhere and threw the lighter. BOOOOM.

It all happened instantly. I don't remember the pain I suffered or how much I screamed, but the smell of my roasting flesh and the sizzle of burning curls has stayed with me. From the center of a quivering swell of fire vapor, from the hallway

[8] *Be! And it is*. What God says of creation in the Quran 2:117.

and window, for a moment I saw all of them. I saw Mom, unconscious in the arms of the very women who had lit the fire in the name of the fight against the vice of pleasure. I saw Dad standing, his body half-burned, surrounded by the very group of revolutionary men who, until several months ago, had called him *Master*; and I saw Beeta and Sohrab who had screamed and screamed until no sound came out and they had fallen silent on the courtyard floor. They all disappeared for one fluttering moment, and then . . . reappeared. Even after all these years it makes me sick to remember how Dad threw himself into the fire to save me and then, with half his body in flames, was pulled out and taken to the hospital. I still remember how Mom, trying to reach Dad and me, had wrenched herself from the greasy clutches of the women who, ladles in hand, had come to scoop their revolutionary fervor and misery onto our quiet happiness.

At the time, I didn't have a concept of death or the afterlife, and I didn't know that every death is a signpost to another life. That's why I was surprised to realize how light I was when my body was still burning and I was looking at myself from above. It didn't take long to figure things out; as soon as I lost my physical abilities, others broadened. I learned which untrodden roads could be taken and, finally, that the best thing would be to give into my family's desire to see me again.

When Dad was first brought back from the hospital, a deathly, terrifying silence reigned over the house. No one went near the basement whose destruction, smoke, and fire had also spread to the courtyard, burning the flowers and trees. The atmosphere in the house with the smoke-stained walls of the basement and courtyard, the bare branches and scorched trunks of the sour cherry and peach trees, was so grief-stricken that even the butterflies and dragonflies of Nowruz didn't flit through our courtyard. Sohrab and Beeta stopped going to school. So, one day, fed up with all the sorrow and mourning,

I began making mischief. I hummed *O lady, lady, lady/ sit on my knee* in Mom's ear as she was silently crying in the shower, and applied Desitin anti-burn ointment to Dad's burnt shoulders when he was sitting on the couch, a tear rolling down his cheek, and I moved Beeta and Sohrab's textbooks around in their bags.

Another time, I put the lid to the pressure cooker in Sohrab's backpack, and Beeta's shoes in the refrigerator. This continued until one day when Mom was lying down, as she so often did those days, so little was the energy she could muster, I began tickling her and, unable to hold back, she let out a long, beautiful laugh. Dad and the children, who for ages hadn't heard any loud noises in the house—much less laughter—came running, and found us with our backs to them sitting on the bed, laughing, and hugging. It was thus that I continued my life alongside my family. Sometimes Mom forgets and, textbook in hand, asks me about school, while Beeta haggles with me over doing the dishes just like before, and Sohrab constantly asks questions about the world of the dead.

I became an enigmatic family rumor. Those who had come to my funeral later questioned their sanity when they saw me cooking with Mom or reading with Dad. That's how Granddad Jamshid's famous saying became the family mantra. He, who sometimes saw me and sometimes didn't, said with a philosophical air, "In this world nothing becomes a reason for anything." And so it was that family, near and far, gradually accepted me as an inexplicable, enigmatic being.

After the "Arab Invasion" which is how Mom always referred to it, we decided to leave Tehran. Beeta was the only one who needed persuading. She still thought if we stayed she would be able to continue her ballet classes and become a great ballerina. Once Dad had shown her enough newspaper and magazine announcements condemning dancing, music and singing by women as being against religious law, she ruefully relented. As Dad said, we could join neither the gangster party nor the new power and the mullahs' honeymoon; we could not be silent bystanders to all the arbitrary, revolutionary injustice and revenge. We couldn't watch as Pahlavi leaders and officials were executed, and political prisoners were broadcast daily on television, pale-faced and stuttering, apologizing to the Great Leader of the Revolution saying, "We were deceived." We couldn't tolerate people who, in the name of anti-bourgeoisie resistance, looted Master Alborz's house then practically gave away his valuable paintings from a street corner or the back of a truck. Once when Dad was passing through Shurabad,[9] he saw a mountain of cassettes and reels of Iranian and international films that had been set alight. It was winter, and as snowflakes melted in the flames, ministry officials whose job was to censor Western products stood around the fiery mountain, hands in their green overcoats that were all the rage among revolutionaries in those years, and reminisced as they pointed at the covers of old Iranian films, laughing.

We'd had enough. Perhaps everyone else could manage. Perhaps everyone else was preparing to increase their tolerance for the events that were becoming increasingly violent and savage by the day. But for us, for our family, enough was enough. They could watch as a pregnant Baha'i woman was thrown from the roof of her house in the name of Islam to the words, "God is great." They could gradually become accustomed to seeing executions moved from inside prisons out into city squares and parks in front of their homes. Putting the stress on the word *wanted*, Dad says most people wanted to get used to everything. As if it were a decision they had made in

[9] A neighborhood in southern Tehran.

advance as they seized their booty, land, jobs, firms, and factories from the enemies of Islam—the affluent and bourgeois—dividing the spoils among themselves and turning overnight from village-dwelling outsiders into salaried Revolutionary Guards and City Council members. It was thus that we decided to sell the house we loved so much, and head to some undecided location towards the forests of Mazandaran where there would be no television, no *Kayhan* newspaper and no gun-toting, *magna'e*-wearing[10] Sisters' Committee, whose ranks had previously been the prostitutes of Shahr-e No[11] and whose new job was the promotion of virtue and the prevention of vice. All we wanted was to disappear in silence from the tarnished page of the city's ever more violent, ever less friendly, and increasingly criminal history.

Early the following summer when the real estate agent came to buy our house for a third of its value, Mom was talking to herself in shock wandering around her favorite spots. She went to the patio beside the half-burnt flowering succulent that reached the top of the living room and to the terrace filled with fuchsia and coleus plants. Sitting on the terrace drinking tea in tribute to the past, she watched the women walking by, now mostly clad in headscarves or chadors. She whispered sadly to herself, "Now women have to put a lid their hair again just like they do with their laughter. Houses and dreams are getting so small that even the butterflies are leaving the city. The walls will get taller again and people will buy thick curtains for their windows. Balconies will no longer be a place for flowerpots, chairs and books, but a storage space for people accustomed to sharing their garbage with others."

---

[10] A type of head scarf that covers the wearer's head, chin, shoulders, and chest which became popular after the Revolution.
[11] A neighborhood in southern Tehran that until the Revolution was famous for its brothels and bars.

While waiting for someone from the real estate agency to come and finalize the deal, Mom sat down on the scorched basement steps and, brushing her hand along the sooty walls, stared into the basement's blackness. Like a banished prophet, she warned, "You killed an innocent child; wait and see how your innocent children will be killed."

We left as soon as we got the cash from the agent. After days of losing our way and finding it again in the forests and on winding, unmarked, and muddy roads, we finally arrived at a village that Dad knew with one look at the calm eyes of the villagers was the place. The safe place where we were meant to be: Razan. From among the areas shown to us by the locals, after sighting the ruins of an ancient fire temple, Mom settled on five hectares on a hill overlooking the surrounding countryside that was serviced by a road so poor and so far from the village that no one had even thought to build there. In fact, no one in the village had ever exchanged land for money. God's land still belonged to the people, and the people, as if offering votive food to a neighbor, gave us those five hectares, saying, "It's God's land. You build it up." Standing on the hill that day, Mom turned towards the ruins of the Zoroastrian fire temple and said, "Just as you did fourteen hundred years ago, we also fled."

And yet, as we laid the first stone for the house near the forest and that ancient fire temple on a hill overlooking Razan, we couldn't have imagined how useless our flight had been given that just nine years later the road leading to the village would feel the weight of a car carrying a mullah and his bodyguards that then ascended the hill to the grove and arrived at our doorstep. I watched them from up in my treehouse and wondered how obscenely they would deliver the news. Mom and Beeta, who had heard the vehicle from a distance, were each waiting in a room to see what it was they wanted this time, now that the house had been emptied of both Sohrab and his books. Smoking his pipe on the porch, Dad stood up, his brow furrowed. The mullah got out of the car. One of the Revolutionary Guards came into the yard and said, "Be at Luna Park Tehran[12] in three days."

Three days later, in a place that evoked childhood games and laughter, popcorn, roasted corn on the cob, and smiley instant photos, Luna Park Tehran was filled with armed Revolutionary Guard patrols and plain-clothes officers equipped with radios, who had shut down the Upside-Down Ship and Train of Terror, to bring real terror to the people's upside-down lives.

More than one thousand men and women in black were waiting for their numbers to be called from noisily crackling loudspeakers mounted on the trees, the Ferris wheel, the Upside-Down Ship, and the Train Station of Joy. The crackling and the foul language of the person screaming into them made understanding impossible. The person bellowing into the loudspeaker said, "Shut up and sit your ass down!" Then screaming at someone else, he could be heard saying, "What, are you deaf?! I said your kid was executed. Here are his things. Now get lost before we arrest you!"

Those, like Dad, who were standing in a corner of the yard anxious and petrified, staring at the number held in their hands, didn't know if they would receive news of a future visit or a bag of clothes from the person cursing and speaking in a loud, boorish voice from behind the loudspeaker. More than half were sitting, beating their heads and crying. Three hours later, Dad was one of those sitting. Instead of visiting times, they had all received a bag and a yelling: "Funerals not allowed and the place of burial is unknown!" Only occasionally did anyone from among the black-clad, sobbing sitters take the

[12] The largest of Tehran's amusement parks prior to the Revolution.

opportunity to say to another, "Our children are either in Kharavan[13] or the desert."

The house filled once again with silence. Just like the time we burned; the *tars*, books, and me.

This time the house's cheery colors themselves began to brood; and there was no need for clothes of mourning. The world turned black. Black trees, black sky, black snow. Snow that suddenly began to fall in the height of summer and did not stop for one hundred and seventy-seven days. Only a month had passed since Mom's unexpected enlightenment in the greengage tree and though she said nothing, she felt everything, sensed it, knew. It had already started to snow when Dad returned home from Tehran with hunched shoulders, and swollen, horror-stricken eyes. That morning the snow had begun to fall so persistently from pitch black clouds that no room for doubt remained for Mom and Beeta. Especially when later that morning, a giant moth appeared and flexed its wings outside Mom's bedroom window; Beeta's left eye was twitching; and a group of crows were kar-karing towards our house. When Beeta saw the moth, she was sure it was Sohrab's spirit come to say goodbye, and yet, both she and Mom ignored these signs. They tried not to feel their effect, but their bodies had become leaden and all motivation was drained from them. And so, they just sat on the porch looking up at the pitch-black sky and wind-whipped snow as it soaked and blackened their skirts. Dad said nothing when he arrived in the middle of the night, frozen and wet. They asked nothing. He took the bag straight to Sohrab's room and then took a hot shower from which he didn't re-emerge for three hours, and then only because of the terrified screams of

[13] An unmarked cemetery south of Tehran where the nameless victims of the executions of 1988 were buried in mass graves.

the villagers whose rooves had caved in under the weight of the snow.

The black snow fell for one hundred and seventy-seven days. The rice in the paddies turned to sludge, fields of eggplants and tomatoes became moldy, and butterfly wings stuck together and rotted. Wet birds starved and cows gave birth to dead calves. We took turns tending the fire in the stove so it wouldn't go out because there was no more oil and the moisture had made the phosphorous match tips crumble. Every day I gathered several loads of wood from the forest in the unrelenting snowfall, carrying them to the porch and watching my family as I came and went. They were blurred and opaque. Three forlorn members of what had once been a self-assured, joyful five-member family. The walls of the house became mildewed and covered in moss; holes formed in the rusty roof. Water dripping from the ceiling into metal pots was the only music in the house as it mixed with thunder and the soft yet constant pattering of snowflakes. And yet, none spoke; not Mom, not Beeta, not Dad, and not the sparrows. The silent wet sparrows that had taken refuge from the forest on our porch.

The weather was misleading. Everything was swallowed by moisture and cold. Our fingernails were wet so much of the time they turned black and puffy. The day we saw that the pages of the books and diaries we had bought again from secondhand bookshops on Enghelab Street had begun to stick together and the ink had run, we were grateful that at least the trunk with our ancestor's writings and books was safe and dry in Tehran. Precisely on the fortieth night, as we all sat in silence around the wood stove and no longer paid any attention to black extremities or empty stomachs, a man with a long white beard and hair, and dressed in a long white robe, knocked on the door, walked past the hunched sparrows without giving them fright and, before we could even stand up, opened the door and sat down next to Dad in front of the wood stove. A vague smile played upon his protruding lips as he held his hands in prayer towards the fire, reciting: *A prayer to you, O fire. Salutations to you, O fire. Truth is the greatest good, it is gladness. Gladness be for him who wants truth for the greatest truth. May the Creator and his created bring to you, O fire, O rays of Ahuramazda, gladness and praise. Be ablaze in this house. Be continuously ablaze in this house. Burn brightly in this house. Be forever increasing in this house. Truth is the greatest good, it is gladness.* We were so intent on our silence that when having said this, the immaculate old man bowed slightly in respect as he backed away and evaporated into the night, before reaching the living-room door, we didn't say a word; we just stared at the fire in the wood stove that had suddenly flared. From then on during all those snowy nights, the fire in our stove never went out and the old man returned every night. Each time he brought several others with him who sat beside us, all wearing the same clothes and reciting the same prayer.

Several nights later when the group of Zoroastrians were reciting their usual fire prayer, our eyes fell on the porch where a villager, too shy to knock, stood cowering with his wife and three children. We opened the door and, as we walked back and forth from room to room to provide them with the last of our somewhat dry towels and clothes, they listened to the fire prayer we had become so accustomed to hearing and that warmed our hearts a little. From that night on, clusters of people from the village, bringing their last pots and pans, blankets, and food were added to the gathering of the men in white, taking refuge in our house—the last that remained standing in Razan. Rooves had given way under the weight of the snow, cows and sheep had died or had fled to higher ground, and the remaining hens and roosters were living in the trees. Some people reported seeing them flying from tree to tree and mating with wild birds. Someone else said he had seen cows and sheep living in caves in the mountains, licking medicinal stones and drinking from hot mineral springs instead of eating grass.

Several weeks later, with no more room to sleep and no more food to eat, the sparrows sensed danger and, spreading their wings, flew from our porch. That day five hungry young men went into the forest armed with bows, arrows, and knives, returning a day later with a sheep, several rabbits, and one hundred sparrows. They proceeded to light a fire on our porch where they roasted their booty and fell on it greedily.

The people grew accustomed to the strange men in white who came every day at precisely the same time, and then disappeared again precisely an hour later. It was by unspoken agreement that everyone remained silent as they entered and listened to the prayer, and spoke loud and fast again as soon as they left. One was looking for a place to sleep, another moaning with hunger, and yet another was looking for her young son who had fallen asleep under who knows which bed or wardrobe. Everyone tried their best to not get into our personal things. But the day Beeta saw her pink ballet slippers on a child's feet, she lost her temper, screaming that she was fed up with all the commotion and so much intrusion. Everyone bowed their heads in silence. After an hour of crying and ranting, she cursed the snooping children, black snow, the people who murdered Sohrab and me, the muddy earth, and the empty refrigerator. When she yanked her shoes off the child's feet and returned to her room, their fast, loud chatter and their fighting over leftovers and sleeping places resumed. It was only Issa, Homeyra Khatun's grandson, who watched everyone, including Beeta, in silence, unaware that years later he would make fiery love to her before cheating on her with Delbar, the blond-haired girl who at that very moment was sleeping just off the side, and whom he would marry and have five children with.

Not long after, with the house collapsing under all the

mayhem, I followed the white-robed men and saw them disappear around the ruins of the ancient fire temple—at the spot where locals believed to be the location of a cemetery for Zoroastrians who had fled Islamized regions centuries ago. I tugged at the robe of the old man who had first come to our house and asked, "What do you want from us?" As though waiting for this question, he answered, "Hope, joy, and prosperity."

All three things had long since disappeared from our home. He vanished then, and neither he nor his companions ever returned.

The sparrows, boars, and rabbits were on the verge of extinction when, on the one hundred and seventy-seventh day, the sky gradually cleared, the black clouds gave way to grey, and the black, wind-whipped snow turned light and soft. By nightfall that evening it had stopped completely. It felt as though our ears, accustomed to one hundred and seventy-seven days of thunder and lightning, the patter of snowflakes, and water dripping into metal pots, were now dulled; not wanting to trust the crowing rooster perched on a tree in the nearby forest, or the chirping of the sparrows that had suddenly burst into song and were flying in the watery sunshine.

Like the first day of Creation, the air was pure and light. The villagers ran out into the yard and embraced one another, yelling and screaming, dancing and twirling in a *chakkeh sama*.[14] But no one could return to their homes in Razan. So much snow had fallen that no earth was to be seen. Again, the people waited. A month later the ground had re-emerged from under the thick layer of snow but was now a giant black swamp that completely encircled our hill and had swallowed everything. Again, the people waited. This time, every day for

[14] A local dance from Mazandaran in which men and women dance in pairs.

twenty days, a group of men set off from the hill down to the valley to test the ground upon which the sun had been shining with all its might. Finally, when the river had resumed its old path, when color returned to the trees, when everything that had been taken from them by the black snow was restored by nature under its golden sun, and the ground under their feet could once again be trusted, the men took the hands of their wives and children and set off for the valley with their last remaining pots and pans, to restart their lives. Not one of them thanked us . . . that's just how it is. Just as they give as one, so they take. Just like the earth. Like water. Like air.

Gradually the hens and roosters with their strange chicks, and the cows and sheep with their newborn young emerged from the forest and descended from the mountain to Razan. The sun slowly cleared the blackness and the green of the plants reappeared. The sound of flutes and song and the shepherd's call travelled once again on the breeze to our grove every afternoon, and earth's last poisonous, black vapor rose to the sky like the ghosts of a vagabond race, and coalesced with the clouds.

I don't know if it was the enlightenment in the greengage tree that made Mom a different person, the one hundred and seventy-seven days of snowfall, Sohrab's death, or the prayers of the white-robed Zoroastrians. Suddenly, she emerged from her shell. She was full of energy, full of ambition, and without the slightest smile on her prominent, still beautiful lips, she leapt around from one side of the grove to the other, from one end of the house to the next, like a wild wagtail popping in and out of wattles, exhausting us with her orders. The black windows had to be washed. The black clothes had to be thrown away and new ones made. Then ragged blankets, sheets, and mattresses had to be separated from the good ones and burned. All of the surviving handwoven carpets from Kashan and Nain had to be brought down from the attic and out of the rooms into the yard to dry under sun; as did all the books, issues of *Ferdowsi, Sepid va Siah, Khushe*, and *Ketab-e Jom'e*, and the *Ayandegan*[15] newspaper that had been sheltered from mice, mullahs, and black snow in attic trunks.

Ruefully separating the damp journals and spreading them out over the surface of the porch in the sun, Dad said, "At least these will be left for your children." Poor Dad didn't realize that, with the exception of memoryless fish, no descendants of his would remain. The walls needed re-painting. The holes in the attic needed plugging with wax and sap. Someone needed to fetch the horses that had fled into the forest and bring them back. Japanese quince, forsythia, sweet viburnum, and roses had to be replanted in the garden. The mildewed walls, rusty windows, and rotting doors had to be repaired. Yet in all of this it was the sound that was unexpected. When the snow stopped and the house's wooden panels began to dry, sounds slowly returned. *Krrt krrt krrt* . . . the termites that had wasted away during the snowfall had come back with a vengeance. They were everywhere: in the furniture, the doors, the windows, the kitchen cabinets, the empty bookshelves, the ceiling. By the time the *krrt krrt* of the termites could be heard issuing from between the wall studs we couldn't take it any longer and realized that, even with all the repairs, the house couldn't be salvaged. It was thus that Dad made the biggest sacrifice of his life. We all breathed a sigh of relief and collapsed on the bare floor when he announced he was prepared to go to Tehran and borrow money from Granddad, or Great Granddad, to completely rebuild the house. But not one of us smiled: for our lips, it was too early for smiles.

Although Dad's words had been reassuring, our money problems were solved much more easily than expected when

---

[15] Various intellectual magazines from before the Revolution.

Effat's ghost came to my treehouse. That very night Effat, whom I had never seen before, came and said that exactly ten steps from the center of the ruined fire temple towards the forest was a stone slab with a turtle carved into it. From there, twelve steps to the south was another stone resembling a chair that could be sat on. Sitting on the rock looking east to where the sun rises a tall, old tree was visible in the forest standing out from the surrounding trees. At a depth of one meter under the south side of the tree an urn of gold left by our Zoroastrian ancestors was awaiting us. When I asked why she was telling me this, she simply said, "Because it is your father who must help the villagers rebuild their houses and a school."

Effat hadn't completely faded into the darkness when I entered the house and handed Mom, Dad, and Beeta each a spade as I woke them up. Several hours later, in utter disbelief and with Dad already thinking about the difficulties of the sale, we had heaved an urn full of Sassanian[16] gold coins and jewels out from among the ancient graves and bones and ceramic bowls, and placed it on the floor of the still-tidy living room. Picking up a gem-studded necklace, Beeta said, "Every meter of earth in this country holds an ancient treasure."

Dad knew that with several powerful mullahs in Tehran and Qom at the helm, the Ministry of Intelligence had confiscated all ancient treasures and quietly imprisoned or disposed of anyone who found them, whilst dividing the spoils amongst themselves. So it was that Dad had no choice but to take the risk and go to Tehran himself to sell it, with the help of Uncle Khosrow and Granddad and Great Granddad. He was fortunate, however, that Granddad and his father treasured Iran's ancient heritage so much that they were prepared to dig into their own pockets, exchanging most of it for part of the family's

---

[16] The last Zoroastrian empire in Iran before the Arab invasion.

estate and their life's savings, before donating it to the national collection, amid much publicity.

Danger persisted, however. We were all worried about the future of these antiquities at Granddad's house, especially since the mayor of Tehran had been offering to buy them. Now, because they had refused all his offers, the mayor had threatened them with the law. Soon after, they received a letter from the mayor's office announcing that the house had to be sold to the city to allow for the construction of a highway. Just the thought of it was a nightmare. We all loved that eighteen-bedroom house with its corridors and entrance gallery, and exquisite wood inlays. It was a part of our family and the country's history. Eventually, Uncle Khosrow, Dad, Grandma, Granddad, and Great Granddad got creative. Uncle Khosrow called a trusted journalist whom he had known years ago. A week later and in the presence of reporters, they donated the Zoroastrian treasure to the national collection, passing it off as collection of family heirlooms. Photographers took pictures of the Achaemenid and Sassanian necklaces, bracelets, crowns, and coins; journalists wrote detailed articles on them. After this, we felt it would not be so easy to steal them, even though we knew antiquity thieves were so closely linked to prominent political, economic, and religious figures. It was thus that early one un-extraordinary morning, when the sun was still working to dry the mud, Razan woke up to the sound of heavy trucks they had hitherto never seen. A line of trucks hauling timber and materials, two trucks of skilled construction workers, and a third laden with books, all led by Dad's car, entered the village.

For six months, the villagers and twenty construction workers from the city labored under the hot sun until Razan became a place that excited the envy of even the urban builders—a place neither Dad nor the villagers ever tired of beholding. A network of streets and alleys separated large, well-built village houses, their walls painted white with natural plaster, lapis lazuli blue, and ochre from the earth. The river now flowed in a stone-lined canal so it would no longer flood easily. Large chicken coops and a bathhouse perfumed with fragrant forest plants, flower-lined streets, fruit trees in the gardens and large paddies with clean, even plots of rice, attracted the stares of every newcomer. It was not surprising that a number of builders fell in love and married enchanting Razan girls. Happy days in Razan had arrived. People worked with renewed hope and energy, relegating memories of their sons unreturned from war to the isolated trunks of their minds as they danced in celebration for their daughters. They built a school; and made ceramics, and wove mats and kilims and cloth, just like their ancestors. In all this development, Dad didn't once think about a road. He didn't want any roads from the city to lead to Razan. If it had been up to him, he would have perhaps even wanted the tire tracks left by the trucks in dirt and mud, grass and meadows, wiped away. Dad hired three of the builders who had married village girls and who were literate to work as teachers. Now from up on our hill, Razan, with all its secrets, memories, and dreams, appeared even more beautiful and prosperous. But though he watched the dizzyingly dynamic life with satisfaction, not once did a smile cross Dad's lips. I was always underfoot, maybe he was wondering the same thing we all were: why had there not yet been any sign of Sohrab?

CHAPTER 6

There was no news from Sohrab because he was waiting. He was waiting for the executions to end. They did end. Some say it was September 27, 1988 and some say it was later. Either way, they eventually came to an end. Five thousand men and women, young and old, whose only crime had been their political or religious beliefs, were killed in the prisons of Tehran, Karaj, Mashhad, and other cities. Once they had all finally died and their corpses had fed the crows and stray dogs in the desert, they didn't sit idle. They set off.

The ghosts of five thousand political and religious prisoners rose up from the cities' deserts and from around Tehran and Khavaran, they looked at their stinking, maggot-infested body parts strewn about and carried in all directions in the mouths of crows and dogs, and then they set off with a common loathing. They wanted to see their murderer's face up close. They could have appeared instantly in Khomeini's bedroom, the man who had signed their execution orders, but memorializing their recently lost lives, they decided to walk in silent accord. It was thus that groups of doleful, unhappy ghosts set off from the southern, western, and eastern deserts of Tehran and converged at the intersection at Vali'asr. Hands in their pockets or smoking cigarettes that some had stolen from passersby, five thousand ghosts marched towards Vali'asr Square, Vanak, Tajrish, and then to Jamaran Street, Khomeini's street. They looked at the men and women who walked right through them without so much as sensing their presence. They looked at the children who could be their own; at crowded stores and streets filled with vendors; at the City Theatre, at Qods Cinema, Sa'i Park and Melli Park. How dynamic life still was without them! How full of cotton candy outside the cinema and fortune-telling with walnuts, how full of boutiques and bookstores and gold sellers. How quickly the boys still fell in love with girls, following them around, and handing them their numbers! How glorious the plane trees on Vali'asr Street still were! How many cats and crows there were in Tehran! Filling their non-existent lungs with air, they wandered until it got dark and then they decided against going to face their murderer. They realized their sorrow was too great for the murder of their murderer to make things any better. Life and death took on another form as they walked on and looked at the faces of the living. Nostalgia and hopelessness filled all of their hearts. Gradually the city fell silent. Lovers emerged from restaurants and cinemas two-by-two, disappearing into the maze of alleyways. Shop lights were extinguished and, here and there, the homeless lit fires around which they gathered. The city streets became empty. The smell of warm food filled the air and the muffled sound of night-time talk filtered out from the windows. Suddenly, the ghosts felt so sad that their constricted throats burst open. Walking north from Vanak Square, five thousand miserable ghosts began to cry. They cried . . . and they cried . . . and they cried. They cried because they missed eating dinner with their loved ones; they wanted herb stew, meat and eggplant stew, and barberry chicken. They missed the carefree laughter alongside their families, their kisses and goodnights. Their tears flowed and flowed . . . until they turned into a torrent.

Here and there passersby who had missed the last buses looked up at the star-filled sky and wondered where the deluge was coming from. It was only the homeless addicts and vagabond lunatics whose inner eyes saw that a river of tears up Vali'asr Street flowed ahead of five thousand despairing, crying ghosts marching like a vanquished army, occasionally leaning against old plane trees and keening in a funereal lament. The flood reached Tajrish Square and Jamaran Street, crossed the bridge over the dry riverbed and flowed under the feet of plainclothes officers. It entered the courtyard and ascended the steps, soaked the rugs and made its way directly to Ayatollah Khomeini's bedroom where it climbed up the feet of his twin bed and reached him as he lay in a fitful sleep at 2:32 in the middle of an ordinary summer night. He was having his usual nightmare. He was dreaming that thousands of family members of people executed had surrounded him in Azadi Square and were ripping and clawing at him with such savagery that not even one drop of his blood hit the ground.

He awoke with a fright and felt the stickiness of his sweat on his fingers, toes, and temples. He rolled over, scratched his long, bushy beard, and when he saw that his baggy shirt, mattress, and pillow were wet, he sat up with a start. He was afraid it was his own blood that had made everything so wet and slimy. He stuck his finger in the moistness and brought it to his tongue. It was salty and slightly viscous. It didn't taste like blood. It tasted like tears. Frightened, he got out of bed and put his decrepit eighty-year-old feet on the wet carpet and sunk into it up to his ankles. He groped around for the light switch and flicked it on. Then he saw that his room was submerged in tears. His heart constricted with the fear of death and he let out a terrifying scream, sending the guards into a panic, bringing the termites who were gnawing away at the wooden ceiling to a standstill, and giving fright to some sleepy Eurasian, collared doves. Eight, usually indolent, guards jumped up and rushed into the house with weapons loaded, and followed the flow of tears from Ruhollah Khomeini's room all the way to Vanak Square, next to the maze of alleyways where the addicts and homeless had fallen asleep under house windows with the lingering smell of warm dinners.

It took three days and nights of diligent, obsessive cleaning before the puddles of tears were all mopped up from the recesses of the house on Rahbari Dead-end off Jamaran Street.[17] He continued to find large puddles in strange places, however, into which he would stick the tip of his right little finger, taste it, and yell out in anger and fear, until 10:20 on the night of June 3, when Khomeini died. Once, when brushing his hand over the mantle in search of his glasses, he found it drenched in tears. He shrieked so loudly that for three days he couldn't talk for the sore throat it had given him cancelled a meeting with supporters among clerical leaders in Qom, and retreated fearfully into a mysterious underground room that was still under construction.

It was thus that at daybreak the next morning after the tear-filled procession, the sorrowful, wandering ghosts each set off alone. Some returned to their families in villages and cities; others remained on the streets of Tehran, paying homage to the aspirations and dreams of the fiery days of the Revolution and in the hope of one day seeing with their own eyes the destruction of the regime that had killed them like flies. And still others were so repulsed by earthly events that they began a quest for transcendence in the spirit world.

Sohrab was among the latter.

---

[17] *Rahbar*: leader.

CHAPTER 7

Doors creaked. Shoes and sandals were thrown into the garden. Pebbles hit the windowpanes. Lightbulbs turned on and off and curtains opened and closed. Before the wide-eyes and terrified gaze of the guards, footprints passed them in the freshly fallen snow and continued towards the yard and steps leading to the house and the door opened then closed. A hand took Khomeini's cloak from the rack and threw it out the window into the yard. Another hand unraveled his turban, put one end of it into the toilet and flushed. In the middle of the night with all the guards searching wildly, and his wife Batoul, in her bedroom saying the Fear Prayer,[18] they could hear footsteps on the porch, voices whispering, and then the cover draped over the chair that was strictly reserved for his Speech Days shifted and sunk inwards as if under someone's weight. One night a young guard was so frightened by the clear voices issuing from under trees and behind bushes all around him, saying, "Murderer . . . murderer . . . murderer . . ." that his finger nervously pressed the trigger, showering the petunias and jasmine with bullets, before the rest of the guards quieted him with their hushes. Even in the middle of the night when Ruhollah's glasses were lifted from the mantel above his head, flipped around and, right in front of his weak eyes, flew to the ground and broke,

[18] A prayer said by Muslims when they feel afraid.

no one in the room with him reacted in the slightest because Khomeini hadn't given any orders.

The man, who in all the years since becoming Supreme Leader of the Islamic Republic of Iran had developed a habit of giving orders as he sat in front of a large mirror, had fallen silent. Sitting in front of the mirror while he spoke with others filled him with such confidence and daring he felt he could conquer the mountains, deserts, and skies and, with the flick of a finger, spread Mohammad's pure Islam throughout the world. Still he insisted on remaining silent. If they hadn't gone too far the night they heaved his sleep-heavy body down from his bed, if they hadn't dragged him the whole length of the room over the hand-woven Kermani carpet and then through the long living room, and tried to propel him off the second floor, his guards would have continued to show restraint. But in the middle of that particular night, Khomeini was so scared and made such a ruckus, that twelve Revolutionary Guards on Jamaran Street also heard his screams and, running into the house, saw his eight special guards pulling, terrified, on his legs as they tried to pull him back into the room. When two Revolutionary Guards shot at the invisible force, the guards finally managed to drag his old, wrinkled body back in through the window. That night when Khomeini realized the others had seen the wet, yellow streaks that ran down his pants, he cried and, for the first time he allowed everyone to see how frightened and alone the man behind that perpetually scowling, stonily arrogant face actually was.

An hour later, the twelve Revolutionary Guards and eight special guards heard him talking in his bedroom. They guessed he was talking, as he usually did, to his mirror. At times his voice was raised to a yell and at times his howling sobs echoed through the old house's rooms that were devoid of sunlight. At noon the following day, when he emerged from his room with sunken eyes, his face covered in sweat, arms and legs shaking, and holding a fistful of crumpled paper, everyone realized that more than just the objects hurled from one end of the room to the other had broken, in that bedroom. The same day, two engineers sat on their knees in front of Khomeini as he ordered the construction of an underground palace. Nobody dared speak against the bizarre plans that he was hurriedly, nervously, and fearfully drawing up right before their eyes. From the very beginning he had said, "Questions suspended."

Contrary to what was published in the newspapers, broadcast on radio and television, and even what was advertised on the twenty-meter-high billboards on Vali'asr, Tohid and Enghelab Streets, many of the soldiers who had volunteered to go to the front were neither militants infatuated with spreading Islam, nor followers of the Revolution and Khomeini. They were just simple-hearted, patriotic young men who didn't want so much as a centimeter of their country to fall into enemy hands. When the ranks of the dead exceeded ten thousand, fifty thousand and then one hundred thousand, the martyrs selected representatives of their own to join forces with the errant ghosts of the executed political prisoners who still sometimes wandered the streets of Tehran in memory of their revolutionary dreams, to finish him off. When they finally came face-to-face with Khomeini in his bedroom in the middle of that snowy January night, their message was clear, "Either you die right now or you build a palace of mirrors, the instructions for which we will give you in fragments, day by day. The day the palace is completed you will die."

It was thus that hundreds of builders began laboring day and night to dig through the basement of the house towards the mountains. Where the engineers gave orders to continue, Khomeini would appear and wave his index finger in the air and scream for them to stop. Where the engineers told them to stop digging because there was risk of a collapse, Khomeini would give confusing instructions and insist that the work continue. It took a year to dig a cavity in the heart of the mountain suitable for the construction of a palace of mirrors; it was several hundred meters square with a height of thirty meters in some places and just one meter in others. However, contrary to what the engineers thought, not only was the job not over, but the most difficult part had only just begun. As the days progressed it appeared the project was taking shape, but it soon became clear that it was becoming murkier by the day. Everyone was confused and worn out, Khomeini most of all. But whereas the workers' drive and desire for money pushed them forward, Khomeini's only motivation was survival as he became increasingly disorientated and older. Meter by meter the structure was built as per the precise instructions fed to Khomeini every minute by the Council of Ghosts comprised of war dead and ex-political prisoners. The palace entrance was formed by a long corridor, narrow and winding, some sections of which were so low the engineers and workers had to crouch down to walk through while others stretched thirty meters into the air. There were mirrors everywhere: on the stairs, on the walls, ceilings, railings, and in the hallways. Broken mirrors on the floor that crunched stubbornly underfoot, their presence impossible to forget for even a moment. There were stairs that ended at sheer cliff walls, hallways that sloped gently upward and converged with the ceiling. Seven contorted floors were constructed in accordance to the whimsy of the Council of Ghosts so that just when the workers thought they were on the second floor, they emerged on the fourth; and when they thought they were going from the fifth to the first floor, they hit a dead end on the seventh. There were windows in the floor, doors, and ceiling. Pillars placed hither and thither were left disconnected from above. Twelve fireplaces were built with only one that connected to the outside; one connected to a bedroom without a door, and the shafts of several converged, whilst the rest led to the mountain. In one bedroom, a second bedroom was built in which there was a third bedroom, in the floor of which was a door that opened onto the floor below but had no stairs. And there were winding, convoluted hallways with destinations that were anyone's guess.

Mirrors. Mirrors were everywhere, catching everyone off-guard with a view of himself from every angle. Gradually fear gripped all who were worked there. Cries of terror could be heard day and night, calling for help out of the labyrinth. Some of the workers said they had seen wounded ghosts without heads or legs in the dark corridors. One day a worker saw the ghost of his martyred brother. The man cried for joy so hard that other ghosts gathered round and wrapped him in their arms to comfort him. Before long, rumor had it that if you were looking for someone from among the martyred or unknown war fallen, the thing to do was get a job there as a laborer. It became normal to hear crying and laughter issuing from within the dark, mysterious interior of the palace. People from all over the country formed long queues in front of the house on Jamaran Street, standing for hours in the rain and snow to join in the work, even without pay, so they could secretly meet with their ghostly loved ones. Later, the guards caught several women disguised as men who had been hired because they wanted to meet with their martyred husbands, make love with them again in the palace's dark recesses, and get pregnant. At first the guards, engineers and Khomeini were happy. They thought the people were full of revolutionary fervor and adoration for its great leader and had come as an expression of their love for him. However, when news of workers meeting with their martyred brothers, sons, fathers and husbands reached the ears of Khomeini and his eight private guards, they began selective hiring. From that point on workers had to fill in long, detailed forms to ensure they had no martyrs in their family. The war ghosts who had found some peace and joy in seeing their families again were angered by this complication. And so it was that one engineer disappeared in a long, dark corridor, never to be seen again. Shortly thereafter, the body of one of the eight private guards was found dangling upside down from a door on the ceiling, his gun sling wrapped around his neck. After that, to prevent anyone from getting lost or disappearing, multi-colored, phosphorescent rope with little bells was strung everywhere. The futility of this became clear, however, when in some places the ropes met, and in others they ran parallel, only to, at some undefined point, came back to where they had begun. Gradually the number of frightened engineers and guards decreased. No one knew if they hadn't returned to work or hadn't returned from it. The last engineer was spotted opening a window facing the mountain wall, where he found himself staring at a mirror five centimeters from his face. When Khomeini, lantern in hand, cautiously peeking into the dark, half-finished corridors, rooms, and stairways, asked the engineer what he was doing, without so much as turning his head, the engineer replied, "I'm thinking about yesterday's work."

This continued for a time and Khomeini was surprised that no one from the government had come to meet with him. Then the reality slowly sunk in. The country no longer needed him. There was no war. No political unrest. All voices had been silenced; everyone had left the streets and battlefields to return to their homes. Now was the time for building. The other politicians could probably organize things themselves. As the days went on, there were fewer and fewer around until Khomeini found himself completely alone and unsettled by the omnipresent mirrors, silence, and darkness. When the last engineer disappeared, no other dared continue. Workers vanished, never to return. Khomeini was eventually obliged to devote a number of hours a day to the construction of his mirrored labyrinth. For the first time in his eighty-seven years, he had no choice but to take a hatchet in his unsteady hands, cut mirrors with diamond blades, saw wood, and sprinkle his wounds with penicillin powder. The first days were tiring, but he gradually became so drawn to his own reflection in the mirrors and the sound of the tools in the silent palace corridors, that he forgot to return home in the middle of the night. The scent of cut wood was bewitching and, for the first time in a thousand years, he recalled that years ago, he had dreamed of becoming a carpenter.

Days and nights and weeks passed, and still he laid stone upon stone, mirror alongside mirror, did the wiring, framed staircases and nailed the steps; he and ate food left throughout the labyrinth by frightened workers tied to phosphorescent, bell-laden ropes. Eventually his connection to the world, politics, and his subordinates was severed. He became self-consumed. Eventually he had made his way so deep into the maze of corridors, mirrors, winding staircases, and half-built rooms, that he no longer found any food because the workers had never set foot in such dark, distant corners.

He reached a point where there was neither electricity nor stairs, neither corridors nor halls, neither rooms nor even walls. It was a vacuum-like place where, when he really thought about it, he realized he couldn't even feel the ground beneath his feet. It was pitch black and the flow of air constricted. No matter how much he groped he couldn't find a wall. Gripped with horror, he realized he'd reached the end of the line. He stopped fighting. Gasping now for breath, he moved his old, hunched body where he thought there should be light and a staircase, but again, found nothing. Occasionally a faint flicker of light in the distance allowed him to catch glimpses of his surroundings. In the dull reflections of the distant light, a fuzzy childhood memory would sometimes spring to life, only to disappear from memory as soon as he took a step towards it. He repeated the names of his grandmother, grandfather, aunts, and uncles aloud to keep his mind alert. Upon reaching his cousins, he suddenly remembered that he had fallen in love with a cousin who was five years older than him, who had crystal-white arms. He was ten when he'd seen her wake up and grope around her mattress for her headscarf, eyes still heavy with sleep. No matter how hard he tried, he couldn't recall ever seeing such a beautiful arm. When she saw him observing her from behind the door, she called to him and started laughing. But he fled—scared and embarrassed. Now, he couldn't, for the life of him, remember her name. He thought maybe it was Aqdas, since her sister's name was Akram. As though in a distant, foggy memory, he recalled with a sense of shame and denial how he had masturbated for the first time, under a thick layer of steam in the shower. Then, walking in the airless darkness and feeling all around to find a wall, he thought to himself that maybe her name was Fatima, since he remembered her brother was Ali.

He moved forward blindly and cursed himself for becoming so old and vulnerable. Then he tried to conjure his cousin's face. She assuredly had a beautiful face; white as snow. Her eyes were blue, or maybe light brown. Either way, he remembered she bore no resemblance to Batul, his wife.

Walking in the nothingness and panting now, he suddenly thought that he had arrived at a door. When he reached out his hand, though, he found himself in front of a smooth, cold mirror. He continued onwards. Somewhere, he had lost his slippers so his feet were numb with cold on the mirrored floor. He reached a place that felt like a corridor; but when he called his name, "Ruhollah," his voice flew out into the darkness, never to return. As he reached out on all sides, he touched nothing; there were no walls. Suddenly his foot hit a step: there was a stairway that descended to a room with no door, but led into another room. Then he passed through many doors and hallways and descended many stairs. He felt many pillars and windows that let in no light, even though they opened, because they had been built facing the mountain.

Once again, he called his name in the inky darkness, "Ruhollllah!" His voice flew out and away again, but this time an echo bounced back. He felt as if he was in a large hall. Then his foot hit steps that led upwards. He walked and walked, through corridors and hallways, up steps, through twists and turns, and rooms, until suddenly, as if awakening from a deep and disturbing slumber, he felt he was back where he had begun: at the darkest point his life had ever known. Windowless. Lightless. When he really thought about it he couldn't even feel the ground under his feet. Now it would be impossible to remember his cousin's name, much less her face. He wanted at least to test his voice again. His voice was still his own. This time, with all his eighty-seven-year-old force, he yelled, "Ruhollllllllaah!" and his voice carried on and on until a childlike echo responded, "Yes?"

A pale light from an indistinct source illuminated the figure of a ten-year-old child leaning against a mirror, looking at him. The child asked, "Who are you?" Then, as though this sight of his reflection in the mirror had restored his strength and self-confidence, Khomeini said, "I am who I am. Someone for whom millions of people voted. Someone who managed an eight-year war. Someone who spread Islam to the far reaches of the earth." The child smiled slightly and said, "Why?" Khomeini said, "Islam must become universal." Again, the child asked, "Why?" "Because Islam is the last and most perfect religion." Again, the child asked, "Why?" Heatedly Khomeini exclaimed, "There are no whys about it! Your understanding has not yet matured, otherwise you would know that this question doesn't have an answer." Calmly but insistently this time, the child said, "But, *really* why?"

His bushy brows furrowed. When his eyes fell on the mirror he became decisive and self-assured again but as soon as he took his eyes from it and looked at the child leaning nonchalantly against the mirror watching him, he felt he was nothing more than a silly stammerer who couldn't even explain his life's greatest goal for which he had thousands killed or displaced. For a moment, the dictator was silent as he probed the depths of the boy's childlike "why." Then, as though understanding something that left him dumbfounded, the knot on his forehead suddenly released. He despaired in these, the last few seconds of his life, that he had no time to explain what he had only just now come to understand. His exhausted heart finally came to a halt, just as his one eye lingered on his own reflection while the other looked at the boy. In that split second, he understood that when delivering monologues he was a fierce ruler, but in dialogue he was nothing but a bearded, illogical little boy, stubborn and pompous. He whispered a single sentence in the last moments of his life: "It took eighty-seven years to understand that the intellectual and logical rules of the monologue are fundamentally different from those of dialogue."

Three months later, his body was found by people who had signed a two-billion-toman contract with his son, Ahmad, before entering the palace. And although they used a satellite GPS, compass, radios, and phosphorescent ropes, it took them three months to find his rotten, decomposed corpse reflected in the mirrors' blackness. In the end, it was the putrid stench that guided them. The same stench that all dictators secrete in the end.

CHAPTER 8

J ust like every dictator, Khomeini died without knowing how his revolution or the Islam it created messed with people's lives; not just the lives of the city-dwellers but also the desert- and mountain-dwellers who would never set foot in a city, who didn't even have roads that led to a city, who didn't have a map to know where the capital was and, even if they had, weren't literate enough to read it.

The Health and Literacy Corps during the Shah's reign had gone to the farthest villages to educate people, but during the Revolution the Revolutionary Guards went to those places to recruit soldiers. The first whiff of danger came in 1979 when the Literacy Corps, which had been coming to Razan for years and whose members were by then practically considered locals—one of them having even married a village girl—went to the city for their annual salaries and didn't come back. Nobody knew what this danger could be, but five teachers leaving and not returning did not bode well. The baby daughter of the one teacher was all grown when, one morning in 1986, the crunching of tires could be heard throughout the village, drawing the sleepy yet terrified inhabitants to the village square to behold one of the five previous teachers entering the village in a muddy vehicle, waving. At first the villagers didn't recognize him. The man was accompanied by three armed men with bushy beards sitting in two Patrols. All were wearing identical green uniforms and had large guns slung over their shoulders. Smiling, the teacher descended noisily from the green Patrol and walked toward the villagers. He shook the hand of one of them and quietly whispered, "It's me, Bahram!" just as one of his fellow soldiers said, "Brother Hossein, are we finally there?" Bahram, whose name was now Hossein,[19] answered, "Brothers, we're here." Then, facing the villagers again, he said, "These are my fighting brothers." The people, confused by his strange appearance and words, asked, "Brother? Fighter?" Clapping an old man heavily on the shoulder, Bahram said, "Fighters in Islam and war! Brothers in religion!" Horrified, the villagers said together, "War?" Hossein looked at them incredulously and said, "The war between *Iran* and *Iraq*? You mean you don't know? The Islamic Revolution? *Imam Khomeini*?!"

In our intentional failure to transmit news of events from Tehran to the people of Razan, word of the Islamic Revolution of 1979 was only now reaching them, seven years later, by way of the teacher-turned-bearded-and-armed-Revolutionary Guard. He also informed them of the other four teachers' fate: one had been executed because of his membership in the People's Mojahedin, another was killed on his first day on the front, the third was a traitor to Islam and the country and had fled abroad; while the fourth, sentenced by a religious judge, had been stoned, together with the woman with whom he'd fallen in love but who had not yet been formally divorced from her husband.

The simple-hearted villagers, whose biggest challenge in life was to co-exist and strike a balance with natural and supernatural forces in the surrounding forests and meadows, were left dazed and confused by this deluge of frightening news. They knew neither how to react nor to what. To the revolution? To

[19] Hossein is an Arabic Muslim name, specifically Shi'a, whereas Bahram is Persian.

Islam? To war, or to the religious laws they had always heard described differently?

Although Hossein's week-long visit with his fellow Guards was nice for his wife and daughter, it did not serve to lessen the people's shock and horror at what had happened in the city during his absence from their village. Briefly Hossein explained that seven years ago people had taken to the streets, chanted death to the Shah and death to America. So, the Shah and his family had fled Iran, His Holiness Ayatollah al-Azmi Imam Ruhollah al-Musavi al-Khomeini returned to Iran from exile in France, the Holy Islamic Republic replaced the tyrannical Pahlavi regime, nighty-eight percent of the people voted for the Islamic Republic of Iran, the leaders of the previous regime were executed, and any remaining opponents of the Islamic Republic were arrested and sent to prison. Ayatollah Khomeini ordered that housing, water, and electricity would be free for the average Iranian, women had to wear a head-scarf, and the Great Leader of the Revolution had ordered all relations with America and all other bourgeois countries cut off. Hossein declared that Iraq had invaded Iran and now all men, young and old, and even children, were on the front fighting to preserve the Holy Islamic State. In the midst of all of this, just once did one old man ask, "Where is Iraq, anyway? And who is America?"

Had Hossein and his companions known that the lamenting voice of the war singer, Kuwaitipour,[20] would so quickly touch the simple, trusting hearts of the villagers as he sang, *Mohammad there were you not/ The destruction to see/ The city once freed/ The blood of your fellow men/ Bore fruit*, that all the young men of the village, whipped into an ecstatic state, would

[20] A singer of epic poetry and passionate war songs that inspired many young men to enlist.

trip over themselves in their rush to stand in line for a sip of
the sweet nectar of martyrdom, they wouldn't have taken the
trouble to spend seven days and nights lauding the achieve-
ments of the Revolution and the Holy Islamic State before the
weak and poor. Kuwaitipour's wailing was so moving and
heart-rending that before the cassette had played twice, dazed,
teary-eyed teenagers, the oldest of them no more than sixteen,
stood in line so that Hossein could give them strips of green
cloth upon which was written, *War, war until victory, O
Sarallah,*[21] *the path to the holy place is via Karbala, and Death to
America*, to tie around their foreheads, and boots too wide that
they were to wear in honor of war until they were removed
from their feet on the day of their martyrdom.

The songs and stories told by Hossein and his companions
of mystical rescues by Imam Zaman[22] on the surface were so
compelling that several of the simple-hearted village boys who
had never even seen a paved road in their lives much less a car,
a city or weapons, believed that if they did their ablutions and
fasted for forty days, they would see Imam Zaman, riding a
white horse, come to greet them, and that he would grant them
their greatest wish. Later, the bodies of three of these
teenagers, already in their second forty-day fast and each
already fifteen kilos lighter, were torn into forty pieces by Iraqi
artillery before their dreams of seeing Imam Zaman and telling
him their only wish was to survive the horrors of war came
true.

For the villagers, the world had suddenly become tainted
and suspicious. Only a few months had passed since Hossein's
return with a bushier beard, a harsher expression, and fellow
soldiers who didn't have time to laude the Revolution or Islam

---

[21] In Arabic, *blood of God.*
[22] The last of the Shi'a Imams whom Shi'a Muslims believe to be in their
midst but who will only reveal himself during the Last Days.

to win over young men and teenagers. From the middle of that rainy night when wet, muddy, irritable, and hungry, they entered the village by way of forest shortcuts, thorns, and swamps, they went straight to each house, banging door to door with the butts of their guns, forcing any male they could get their hands on into their muddy Patrols at gunpoint, and carting them away. After the sounds of the first bullets rent Razan's peaceful night and fear tore through the hearts of the people, there was a sudden silence. The sparrows didn't stir; dogs hid their tails between their legs and cowered behind houses. The crests of roosters drooped, and the udders of cows and sheep dried up in fear.

From the moment that Hossein and his companions first set foot in the village—taking us and everyone else by surprise—and their return several months later, there was not a young man left in the village who could shoulder the weight of a gun. The only exceptions were those who had gone into hiding in the forest with the help of women, their whereabouts unknown to everyone except the women, who occasionally went to meet them and came back pregnant. Issa was one of those young men whose grandmother helped him flee into the forest to wait out the war. Another was Sohrab.

We had come all this way to escape Tehran—we had sought refuge here. And so our despair was greatest. All our dreams of life in a safe, tranquil environment dissolved the minute Hossein and his gang arrived. They came to the house unannounced to take Sohrab but, having just managed to send him into the forest minutes before, we denied his existence. Their expressions clearly showed Hossein and his gang didn't believe us; at the time, we still believed there was a chance. But there wasn't.

Nobody knew when this insatiable war, fought with the flesh of child mine-sweepers, would come to an end. Women prayed they would only have girls, or not fall pregnant until it was over, because no man who left ever returned. Not even their bodies. It wasn't until a year after the forced recruitment that a group of chador-clad women and armed men from the Martyr and Veteran Foundation came to the village—sent by Hossein. They arrived with several sacks of rice, cans of vegetable oil, and wall clocks, to meet with families, who greeted them with smiles, tea, and sweets before they were told their children, brothers or husbands had been martyred. No sooner had the villagers placed a sweet in their mouths than the envoy thoughtlessly blurted out, "Spread the good tidings that your children have risen to join the Fourteen Immaculate Imams!"[23] The shock was so great the people didn't know whether to swallow the sweet or spit it in the faces of these bearers of ill tidings. They cried. They wailed, they clawed at their cheeks and donned clothes of mourning. The world, so full of color before Hossein's arrival, was suddenly black. But, though the employees of the Martyr and Veteran Foundation turned their bags and car boot inside out and upside down in search of the martyr plaques for the families, they eventually realized that they had completely forgotten to pack them. Hurriedly, they asked for the provisions back, telling the families they had come by mistake and leaving them the wall clocks and an apology. With that, they leapt into their vehicle and sped away as fast as the track would allow, disappearing through the bushes and trees. It was years before Hossein would show up again in Razan, and then it was with chainsaws.

Only the clocks from the Martyr Foundation hanging on walls of devastation remained to remind the people with every tick tock of the second hand, that even with the passage of time, even though all clocks in the village chimed in unison, nothing would bring their men back.

---

[23] The twelve Shi'a Imams plus the Prophet Mohammad and his daughter, Fatima. In Shi'a belief, these fourteen individuals are immaculate and without sin because they were sent by God.

Several months later, at exactly 9:24 and 3 seconds on an ordinary morning in 1988, just as a sad man with a sack of martyr plaques slung over his shoulder entered the village, all the clocks from the Martyr Foundation went to sleep.

Even though it was years before Hossein would set foot in Razan again—not even coming to see his wife and daughter—his shadow did not fall far from the village. Shortly after Hossein and his gang's forced recruitment and the hapless arrival of the Martyr Foundation employees, the dream of a village child came to pass. A mullah climbed out of a military jeep in the village square and, holding a large metal megaphone, entered the *tekyeh*[24] and soiled the steps of the *saqa nefar*[25] with his muddy shoes. Then, facing the village, he blew several times into his megaphone and yelled, "People of Razan, raisers of martyrs, your attention please! People of Razan, raisers of martyrs, your attention please! . . . The Great Leader of the Islamic Revolution has decreed that all books, music cassettes, and recordings of speeches must henceforth be examined to ensure the eradication of anything that runs counter to the Revolution or Islam! All villagers are therefore obliged to hand over any books or cassettes they have in their houses immediately so their Islamic nature can be verified!"

The villagers, whose heartstrings had snapped with each refrain of "raisers of martyrs" and the thought of their children who had not returned from war, upon the mention of books looked unconsciously towards our house; the very house whose inhabitants had been drawn to Razan along invisible

[24] A religious space where *taz'ieh* plays are performed, a type of passion play re-enacting the deaths of Hassan and Hossein at Karbala.
[25] In Mazandaran, a religious place located next to mosques or *hossainiyas* (halls for Shi'a commemoration ceremonies), usually dedicated to Abu Fazl.

paths in 1979 on a misty morning with hopes of sanctuary and serenity.

On the only hill overlooking the village, our newly built house always invited stares from newcomers, and it was certainly not spared their gaze—perhaps it was the very reason they had come. Just as they had done before, they entered our grove and house unannounced. But we had heard their megaphone and just had time to shoo Sohrab into the forest with two bags of books on politics. Minutes later their muddy boots were dirtying antique handwoven carpets. Without so much as a glance through the remaining books, they dumped them all into sacks and hauled them away. It wasn't until they were back in their jeep that, again without even looking at Dad, the mullah said, "Be at the square in an hour."

With the exception of Mom, who was not willing to put on a headscarf to leave the grove, all of us were in Razan's square an hour later standing alongside the villagers and looking at the mullah who stood in the back of the jeep, wheezing and screaming into his superfluos megaphone, "Misguided books! Books against God and against the Quran! Books against the Revolution!" Wrenching Dad's books out of the sacks several at a time, he threw them to the ground and continued, "The Great Leader of the Revolution has ordered a cultural revolution! We must not allow satanic books to poison the minds of our simple-hearted people!" Then, together with the other Revolutionary Guards, he hurled the books by the armful into the middle of the square. One Guard who was younger than the rest, nonchalantly brought a gallon of petrol from the vehicle and emptied it over them. The Guards stood, guns cocked, surrounding the books and facing us, the people. I looked at Dad who had turned red in the face; the sound of his grinding teeth hurt my ears, and I looked at Beeta, squeezing Dad's hand and biting her nails. As the young Guard, whose mustache hadn't even begun to sprout, dumped petrol over the books, a collective sigh rose up from the villagers who, though knowing neither how to read nor write, had heard the books' innocent lamentations. Worried, everyone turned to look at Dad who had their trust and affection from the moment he had arrived.

As the mullah shouted unnecessarily into his megaphone, perhaps in an effort to make the lizards in distant forests swell with his anger and hate, he stared at Dad and said, "We have produced martyrs . . . We had a revolution . . . We swore on the Quran that we would protect the pure blood of the martyrs and would not allow the enemy to penetrate our houses . . . or the Devil to infiltrate the minds of the simple-hearted. In the name of the Great Leader of the Revolution I will set these perverse books alight to serve as a reminder that, just as was said at the inception of Islam, we need no book other than the Holy Quran to guide and deliver us from devils!"

And so, with a slow sweep of the arm that remained forever etched in my memory, he took out a match, lit it, and tossed it onto the pile of books. With a quiet *huff . . . ff . . . ff* the flames rippled over the pages, catching first the old books with the brown paper whose smell I loved so much. I vividly remember how *Danko's Burning Heart* was engulfed in flames that then licked at Luce's skirt who, desperately trying to protect herself from the fire in the pages of Romain Rolland's book, held Pierre tightly to her breast. I watched as the fire spread to the intertwined lovers Pierre and Natasha, Heathcliff and Catherine Earnshaw, Scarlett O'Hara and Rhett Butler, Elizabeth and Mr. Darcy, Abelard and Heloise, Tristan and Isolde, Salaman and Absal, Vis and Ramin, Vamegh and Azra, Zohreh and Manuchehr, Shirin and Farhad, Leyli and Majnun, Arthur and Gemma, the Rose and the Little Prince, before they had the chance to smell or kiss each other again, or whisper, "I love you" one last time.

Oh! . . . Remedios the beauty and her white bedsheets, the

fragile yellow wings of Mauricio Babilonia's butterflies and the constant groaning of Huckleberry Finn's paddles in his wooden boat merging with the flames, burning, and disappearing as if they had never existed. It seemed as if human beings had never needed love or truth, never needed history or wisdom, never needed adventure or knowledge. It seemed as though humans didn't want anything . . . Maybe they just wanted silence; a refuge from the hoards who wouldn't even leave the inhabitants of Mazandaran's distant forests in peace—a place they say resisted the Arabs' sword in the early days of Islam for two hundred years . . . Maybe all that we humans needed was a cozy corner safe from the violence and oppression and ignorance of others. Just like Dad, whose grinding teeth were still tearing at the veins of my soul. The flames surged, lighting up the bearded faces of the mullah and the three Guards standing closest to the fire, to warm themselves. Nobody said anything. Not the mullah. Not even the people; and not Dad. The flames engulfed the hard- and softbound books with such a *huuufff . . . ff . . . ff* that all eyes were riveted.

Will Durant's eleven-volume *The Story of Civilization*, the five books of *Philosophy by Plato*, Juvaini's *History of a World Conqueror*, *The History of Beyhaqi* and Tabari, the *I Ching*, and *The Idiot* were burning together with *One Hundred Years of Solitude*, *Nina*, *Rebecca*, *White Fang*, and *How the Steel was Tempered*. I heard lone Rebecca's cries and Colonel Aureliano Buendía's protests saying to Ursula with disgust, "Even in all of my tyranny, never did I do this." I saw *The Gadfly*'s Arthur Breton marching again and again against the priest and the church regime, not giving up his struggle despite the conflagration. *Animal Farm* was burning: the cows, donkeys, pigs, dogs, and horses braying and squealing; the odor of their roasting flesh filling all of Razan. But the mullah and his three companions felt nothing.

The Old Man and the Sea, *The Little Black Fish*, *Talkhun*, *Ulduz and the Crows*, *East Wind: West Wind*, *The Iliad* and *The Odyssey*, *Antigone*, *For Whom the Bell Tolls*, *Hamlet*, *The Divine Comedy*, *The Waste Land*, *The Red and the Black*, *Zorba the Greek*, the *Mahabharata*, the *Gulistan*, the *Masnavi*, Hafez, Hallaj, *Crime and Punishment*, *The Stranger*, *The Prince*, *The Blind Owl*, *The Castle*, *The Last Temptation of Christ*. All those voices, those books, each of which was part of the body and soul of our five-member family: our arms, our hearts, our hair, our dreams, our eyes, our mouths. With the burning of Dad's *tars*—which had been our ears, mind, and soul—then of me, and now the books, we had also lost both our limbs and our voice.

We couldn't bear the wailing of Shakespeare and Rumi, Hafez and Confucius, Zoroaster, Buddha, and Khayyam any longer, so we set off towards the house. En route from the village square, towards the alley and up the slope to our grove, I saw with my own eyes how clumps of Dad's hair had turned grey. For seven days after that, no one in the house said a word. Standing on the porch as the fire and smoke from the books filled the valley, and the breeze spread far and wide the burnt smell of *The Feather* by Matheson, even Mom cried. Meanwhile, Sohrab was keeping watch from atop a distant tree. The house had abruptly become devoid of cheer. It became silent. Empty. Hollow.

After a week of silence, it was Dad who entered the living room with an arm full of four four-hundred-page notebooks and black, blue, and red Bic pens. He told us that we needed to begin writing. We looked at him as if he'd lost his mind, but out of respect we took the notebooks and stared at him, as he explained, "Write. Write all you remember. The characters in novels, their loves, wars, peace; their adventures, hates, betrayals . . . Write down anything you remember from the books."

And so we did. From morning to night for forty days; all any of us did was write. Days passed and we sat in a silent depression, our pens pressed against our foreheads trying to think where and from which books to begin. Gradually characters came to life; adventures, loves. With the resurrection of characters and authors, poets and philosophers, mystics, composers, and painters, voices and tunes, murmurs, whispers, and laughter slowly made their way back into to the house. Once again, our home was filled with a bit of poetry and light. Music and verses of hope returned. Beeta remembered some Rumi and excitedly recited:

Not of righteousness nor ruined drunkards are we
Neither here nor there to say where are we
Like Hallaj not afraid of the gallows are we
Crazed in knowledge of love, Gods are we.

Sohrab remembered some parts of *Animal Farm* and wrote, *All animals are equal but some animals are more equal than others.* Then Mom recalled a quote from Scarlett O'Hara and said, "After all, tomorrow is another day." And Dad wrote a passage by Charles Baudelaire: *One should always be drunk . . . But with what? With wine, with poetry, or with virtue, as you choose. But get drunk.*

Although from that day until Sohrab's surprise arrest, a window of joy and hope had opened in the house, even though we knew how delusory Dad's wish to record those great works in cheap, four-hundred-page notebooks was. Day and night, our heads bent over the paper, writing outlines of novels, histories of ancient Iran, mystical and philosophical ideas, and verses from great poets, we watched as a sense of hopelessness seeped into the very cells of our being. Even with each word committed to paper we understood that, contrary to what Dad believed, culture, knowledge, and art retreat in the face of violence, the sword, and fire—and for years after remain barren and mute. Perhaps it was just like those years that became known as the Two Centuries of Silence.[26]

---

[26] A reference to the scholarly book by the same name written by Abdolhossein Zarrinkoub, that relates the events and circumstances of the region after the Arab conquest of Persia in the 7th century AD.

CHAPTER 9

The mothers thought, *If we die they call our lone, defenseless children orphans, but when our children die, nobody calls us lone, defenseless mothers anything.* It was thus that they began calling themselves 'orphan mothers'. Mothers who had been orphaned by their children.

Just as the hapless arrival of the Martyr Foundation employees was beginning to fade from its memory, Razan's seemingly calm and beautiful heart suddenly stood still when it found itself the sudden home to a large graveyard. A graveyard the breadth of memories, hopes, and dreams; a graveyard the length of the past, present, and future. In the days and months after the storm of black snow and the end of the war, there was no news from veteran soldiers and nobody came from the provincial capital or Tehran to help the inhabitants of Razan, or even remembered their existence. If Effat's ghost hadn't come to my treehouse and to their rescue with the Zoroastrian bequest, Razan would still be no more than ruins. The war was over and those who came back from the front were vying for jobs and their share of the spoils. They didn't have time to think of villages, especially a village so remote it didn't even appear on a map of the country; where only gadabout birds and lovelorn people ended up. Among congratulatory news of new posts, inauguration ceremonies, purchases, and sales, and the demolition and construction of urban properties, the only news Razan received was of the killed, the lost, and the prisoners of war.

It was during this time that one day, a man with sad eyes and a large backpack entered the village. He thrust his two big fists into the pack, handed the rusted plaques to the Second Soothsayer, and just as he had come without saying hello, so too he made to leave again, without saying goodbye. But abruptly, the Soothsayer, who remembered him from years before, asked him why he was going through all the trouble of delivering the plaques. The owner of those sad eyes, who didn't think anyone in the area would still remember him, said, "The story is longer than you have patience for," and he continued on his way. The Soothsayer followed him, however, with slow, steady steps, and handed the stranger a hand-rolled cigarette saying, "Now your eyes are just as sad as the one you killed." The stranger stopped. He wasn't surprised to hear it. He smoked the cigarette calmly, then crushed the butt underfoot. With the Soothsayer still beside him, he took a step forward. Then turning around, he said, "Sometimes an inheritance is passed not from father to son, but from one fool to the next."

The people didn't know what to do with the rusted plaques. They had just finished celebrating the construction of their new houses and the marriages of their daughters. Perhaps it was true what they said: that every marriage is followed by mourning. Their young sons had been taken from them, and in return, they had received a piece of iron. And so they set off for a large expanse of land with the last object they had by which to remember their sons. Each of the mothers dug a hole and placed a piece of clothing, a shoe, a cloth, or wooden doll inside, covered it with earth, and, together with the small gold bells that were traditionally tied around children's ankles so they wouldn't get lost, wrapped the plaques around a sapling and planted it over the grave. Years later, among the pink and white silk thread blossoms of the pink siris and their intoxicating perfume, the plaques and bells would help the mothers remember Razan's young men; *ding-a-ling, ding-a-ling . . . we are still running around you with wandering feet*. None of the mothers realized it would never come to that, nor that one day in the not so distant future, they would join their sons.

It was the youngest great grandchild of the village leader whose five-year-old eyes first fell on Roza as she crossed the village square, her head uncovered, and wearing a floral house dress that fell just below her knees. She walked without seeing anyone. The villagers were frightened. Some thought Sohrab's death had made her crazy. Others thought she was sleepwalking because her steps were slow and steady and she looked nowhere but straight ahead.

When the old men saw Roza walking to the edge of the village without a headscarf and wearing a floral dress, they thought it best not to interfere and so continued sipping their tea in the coffee house. There was nothing at the end of the village road. No village, no house. Just forest. An endless forest that merged with deep, humid woodlands said to be places of no return. Roza hadn't gone far from the village square when the only young man of the village to come under the influence of Hossein and his gang's talk of Islam during the war and who considered himself a Basiji, thought to go after her to remind her that in an Islamic country she had no right to go about looking like that in front of strange men. The young Basiji had taken no more than a few steps when he saw one of the orphan mothers take off after Roza. The woman knew neither where nor why she was going. She only knew she had to go; that it was something she had wanted to do for a long time. A power kept her from looking around or back at the house where, until not so long before, she had lived a life of poverty, together with her now-martyred son. They were just leaving the village square when the rest of the orphan mothers, one by one, eagerly followed. The villagers were confused. Their husbands ran after them, hoping to save them from their madness but, without even the faintest of smiles on their lips, the orphans continued in the direction of the deep Mazandaranian forest. This is the place, they say, where luminous blue butterflies that have never seen light illuminate the way for the lost; the place that was still occupied by innocent, ancient forest spirits.

The village men quickly set off after them but, after three days and three nights of walking in the humid, mossy forest, they had found no trace of the women. The men split into several groups, but none could find so much as a single footprint. It seemed as though all the orphan mothers had become the moss clinging to the tress in the ancient Hyrcanian forest, or the luminous blue butterflies that fluttered ahead of the men the whole way—as if trying to distract them from their search with the blue-gold dust they sprinkled on the searchers' heads and shoulders. It felt as though they had become the cool morning breeze that caressed the men's faces and arms through the morning mist to wake them up and continue their quest in the forest, whose trees were so high and canopy so dense that no sunlight penetrated to the forest floor. Gradually the ground turned swampy and the men sunk deeper with each step. Leeches latched onto their arms and legs, and legless lizards slithered between their feet, as though tickled by the flow of cold water.

After three days of walking non-stop at dawn on the fourth day, the mist parted in front of the villagers' tired, hungry eyes just enough for them to look with horror upon the last surviving Mazandaran tiger of the Hyrcanian forest. The giant young beast with sorrowful eyes looked at them as if he understood their pain. With the only gun he had been given by Hossein and his gang to defend Islam and the Revolution against an attack from the People's Mojahedin, the Basiji boy took aim. The Soothsayer quickly stopped him before the trigger could be pulled and instead, approached the tiger quietly and respectfully. To the astonishment of the weary men, both seemed to confer and then disappear into the trees. An hour later, the Soothsayer returned and said that the tiger had come to express his condolences for the loss of their wives and to warn them that they could not venture further into his dark, silent realm. Just as he had stopped searching for his mate years ago, so too would their search be in vain.

When the villagers, their heads bowed, turned around to go back to the village, the Basiji, who had been the one to kill the tiger's mate a few years before, fearfully ran ahead of the others. When the first night turned into morning, he was nowhere to be found. There was not even a body. They only saw his gun which had been thrown up high onto a tree branch, its barrel crushed by the tiger's teeth and its stock gnawed through. The villagers did not quicken their steps nor did anyone mention the young Basiji ever again.

Contrary to what the people believed, however, it wasn't the tiger that had ripped the Basiji to shreds. No one but the Basiji, himself, knew that it was the forest jinns who had punished him for breaking the laws of nature by senselessly killing the last female tiger in the Mazandaranian forest—the only female tiger that hadn't had the chance to reproduce and thus ensure the continuation of its species, stretching back millennia. The night before, with blood from his wounded neck dripping on the fog, the young Basiji recalled how several years before, he had shot the pregnant animal in the neck, and how, her chest still heaving with frantic breathing, he ripped off her beautiful skin, salted it, and laid it under the hot summer sun to dry.

All of the ancient books say that jinns take an eye for an eye. So, it was no surprise when he was skinned that night by twelve forest jinns, and his skin salted and laid out to dry in the hot summer sun the following day. The young Basiji saw how those wandering jinns ripped his flesh and bones into pieces and took them to Razan where they were dumped in front of the village dogs, just as the Basiji himself had done with the flesh and bones of the pregnant tiger, before boasting about it to the other village boys. Dead, the Basiji watched as the dogs lunged at his flesh, then ripped and devoured it. An hour later just one dog, a dog that lived in their neighborhood, expelled what he had eaten, next to the canal behind the Basiji's house. It wasn't long before the dog's excrement had turned into fertilizer, from which a fresh, fragrant bush of wild chocolate mint sprouted. One day when the Basiji's mother went to the canal behind the house as she always did, she picked several wild chocolate mint stalks, then crushed them together with garlic and a pinch of salt, and mixed it into a bowl of yoghurt. The old woman, knowing nothing of the turn of events, teared up at the thought of her son as she ate her delicious yoghurt and herbs. Looking up to the sky, she gave a deep sigh, and said, "Oh how I miss my son. May God have mercy upon him. He loved yoghurt with herbs." From that day forward, the Basiji realized that God had forgiven that little fragment of his being over which his mother had prayed, but not the rest of him, which was still cursed by the tiger and the forest jinns—no, never!

Several days later while the grass, flowers, fungi, and dried forest leaves were being crushed underfoot by the orphan mothers; and spores, butterflies, and dragonflies were flutter-ing in the air around their heads, the men returned to the vil-lage. The mothers were not thinking about anything. They just walked, day and night. When the luminous blue butterflies laid eggs, the bird spiders spun their webs in their hair, and the dragonflies bit their earlobes, they noticed nothing; and when they drank from the springs, alongside the squirrels, foxes, and flowers they didn't see them. They didn't even see the tiger, who roamed around them every night, like a protective spirit. They let the wandering forest spirits of old make noise around them at night and the forest jinns boast. They let the monsoon rains soak them, and the whirling leaves engulf them. They didn't pay attention to anything because they only had eyes for their martyred sons walking ahead of them, little bells tied to their ankles. Where their sons sat, they also sat. Where their sons drank, they also drank. Far from cities, they passed villages and summer pasturing grounds; and with each village and every meadow they walked through, their numbers decreased. Perhaps among strangers the women lost both themselves and their tortuous memories. Perhaps weak and fatigued, they fell prey to jackals and carnivorous moles. Perhaps they stopped and turned into tree trunks to die in memory of their sons, standing, covered in moss and leaves and fireflies. Who knows? Perhaps they simply went with their sons up the highest tree and joined the shadows of the stars and sad forest spirits. They walked and walked and walked, until one day Roza found herself alone.

She was the only woman in the group who had been alone from the start. She had never seen Sohrab walking before her or settling down for the night. She had left because she wanted to lose herself. She didn't want to sit in her newly rebuilt house and look at the freshly painted walls, and the new furniture and carpet, and imagine how Sohrab was killed or how I suffered as I burned. She didn't want to think about the future and what other calamities might befall Beeta and Hushang. She wanted to run away from herself, from her fate. She didn't want to be where ever she was. She vaguely wanted to attain the state that she had experienced only once before atop the greengage tree. She wanted to see herself from above, from afar.

It was thus that she continued non-stop for days and weeks, until one ordinary and pleasantly sunny midday, in the lush green mountains far away from the world and forest and people, she finally stopped. She didn't know where she was.

Maybe she had reached Azerbaijan or Kurdistan. After months, she finally felt the heat of the sun on her skin whilst a breeze ruffled her web-covered hair that, at night, was illuminated by baby fireflies. She sat under a Persian ironwood whose leaves had been turned red, yellow, and orange by autumn. She fell asleep right there and re-awoke after who knows how many days with a hand gently shaking her shoulder. She forced her eyes open and saw a shapeless blur. It appeared to be a traveler. A traveler with a large backpack, a sunburnt face and blue eyes. He said he had spent years wandering around the mountains and forests and meadows of Asia. He didn't ask Roza anything, not even why someone who looked so young could have such completely grey hair. He spoke of himself. He said he had been totally consumed by the forests of Iran for two years and during this time had learned Persian. He talked constantly as he erected his tent and placed skewers of potato and corn over the fire. He said he'd learned the meaning of life from the yogis in the steppes and mountains of India; and how to ride a horse and understand what it meant to be one with nature from the nomads in the green meadows of Kyrgyzstan. From the people in the snow-capped Pamirs in Tajikistan he had learned how to make do with little. With dervishes in Pakistan and Iraq he had learned how to turn the eye inward, and in Iran he had discovered the vastness of the desert's ancient silence.

After weeks and months of silence, he spoke so much that words gradually found a place in her mind and became meaningful again. Her extreme desire for silence had left her lips and tongue swollen and dry. The man's words slowly brought her back to the world of the living. Her eyes, seemingly dried in their sockets, became moist again. After months of immobility, her eyes once again looked from side to side. She saw the man and gradually remembered herself. She got up. Horrified, she wondered that if she were still Roza, then where were

Hushang, Beeta, and Bahar? She looked at her feet. They were still shoeless, and her toes and heels were scratched and chapped.

She sat down and took her right foot in her hand. She was just beginning to remember the sensation of pain when the traveler sat down next to her with two metal bowls and a piece of bread. He didn't insist she use her vocal cords. Perhaps after weeks of silence and solitude it was enough for him just to see someone he could practice Persian with. Once Roza had licked the bottom of her bowl, she cautiously held it out to him. She wanted it filled again. He had already laid out his sleeping bag and was snoring as she ate. With a faint spark of memory, Roza looked at the fire and then the sky. The stars were low and, as she fell asleep, she wasn't sure if it was their light that was warming her or the fire's last flames.

Days and weeks passed. Occasionally, Roza would stop to ask herself if it were really she, who was following this man over mountains and deserts? A man who at the earliest opportunity procured a sleeping bag, pants, boots, and a warm jacket for her. A man who at night would smile at the tiny winking lights in Roza's hair before saying goodnight; and in the morning, would get up earlier than she and do yoga for a long time before preparing breakfast. A man who, just like her, had no desire to count the days or know in which region of which province or country they were. A man who only wanted to be lost in the heart of nature, far from people. Just like herself.

During the first days, the man was constantly testing his Persian and was very talkative. One day, he suddenly stopped talking. He assumed silence with such calm and tranquility that Roza didn't mind at all. Day and night, they enjoyed eating together, walking together and watching the sun rise and set, in silence; until one day, they realized they had accidentally entered Turkey. Imagining that they had inadvertently entered another country by walking through the mountains in a world where people get killed just for having a toe over one side of a border or another, they laughed so hard that tears flowed from their eyes; and a little off to the side, the traveler unzipped his pants and urinated, so that he wouldn't wet himself. And so it was that after the long silence, laughter became the common chapter in their relationship. From that day onward, they would burst out laughing, just by exchanging glances in silly situations. They felt so free in the mountains of Turkey that one day, without even taking notice of her, the man took off his clothes and dipped into a hot spring they had found. Until then, the only man Roza had ever seen naked was Hushang, and even then, only in the pale light that shone through the window into their room. She felt distressed at this, reliving many distant memories. She looked at her hands as they stirred their lunch over the fire, and thought that until now, these hands had only been accustomed to preparing food for members of her family. She looked at her boots, her sleeping bag, her sweatshirt and jacket, realizing that she had never had anything like them before. Once again, her eyes fell on the man's body in the distance and, suddenly shamed, a warm, familiar feeling shook her whole body. Trembling, and with face flushed, she got up and fled from their camp. That evening the traveller found her between two large, flat rocks beside the river where excessive crying, screaming, and self-flagellation had left her unconscious.

During the night, Roza woke up to find herself next to the man in his tent, surrounded by the sound of the flowing river. Her body was exhausted, and when she felt her cheeks the wounds left by her nails hurt, yet she was calmed by the poetic light emitted by the fireflies in her hair under the low-slung tent. It felt as though the physical pain she had inflicted on herself had somehow alleviated the psychological pain. She felt like a balloon that had suddenly been deflated. She could feel the heat from the man's body asleep next to her in his sleeping bag. She wondered how many months she had walked with him; she didn't even know his name. She just knew that he was Italian and that his father had been a mountaineer who had frozen to death in the Alps, and that his frozen body had been found years later, by shepherds.

She closed her eyes and smelt something familiar. The warm, pleasant fragrance of trust. She rolled over so she could see the man's face. When she saw the sleep-slackened lines on his face, and his long, salt-and-pepper beard that moved slightly with each breath, she realized that she had never seen a man's face before. There was a faint smile on his lips that made Roza suddenly wonder if he was awake and just pretending to be asleep. With this thought, her whole body was enflamed with shame and she quickly sunk into her sleeping bag, the sound of his steady breathing making her body go limp with desire. She was uncertain about her faithfulness to Hushang. It had never been put to the test. She was disgusted with herself. Sinking deeper into her sleeping bag, she fell asleep, thinking of her husband.

It was still in the depths of the night when she awoke with a start. Maybe it was a cuckoo singing nearby or an owl that had woken her. She stuck her head out of the sleeping bag and looked at him. He was still sleeping like a child; he hadn't even rolled over. She wanted to touch his salt-and-pepper beard. She summoned up the courage to touch it. His beard was soft and so long it was about the same length as her own hair. She felt her own hair. After months of walking in the sun, the wind and the rain, with spider webs and insect eggs and fireflies in it, her hair had become rough and knotted. She got up and found some shampoo, soap, and a new set of clothes among the things he had bought for her. She went down to the river; the air was warm and the water cool. When the cold from the water had filled her entire body, no matter how hard she thought, she could not recall the last time she had bathed. She let the cold, clear water wash her hair, tickle her still youthful, bare breasts, and grab at her buttocks. An unprecedented urge made her apologize to all the eggs and creatures who had nested in her hair and had been her travel companions all of those months, as she surrendered them to the river. When she emerged from the water, it was still dark. The warm sleeping bag relaxed her body. She crouched down and let the clean fragrance envelope her. No matter what she did she couldn't fall asleep. She wondered what was wrong with her. She rolled over again and looked at the man. Her face was so close to his that she could feel his breath. For the first time the man's shapely lips, his eyelids and long forehead appeared beautiful to her. She wanted to look at him until she fell asleep, but as if sensing her scrutiny, his eyes slowly opened.

Later, when she went over those moments again and for the hundredth time, she was embarrassed that her open eyes so close to his own, hadn't frightened him. For many long minutes, they looked at one another. It was Roza who finally reached out and brushed her fingers against his cheek and caressed it. A completely unknown feeling took hold of her spirit and body, making them alert and bold. She didn't want to give in to her fears, her embarrassment, or her worries. For the first time ever, she felt as if she didn't have a past. She reached out and embraced the man; and the man's still young, hard body welcomed her. They wound together and the sweet, warm fragrance of trust, along with soft breathing that then came faster and faster, transforming the tent's low ceiling into the beautiful expanse of the mountain night sky. They kissed and caressed each other, Roza allowing his experienced, masculine hands to explore every inch of her body, to smell, to kiss, and devour. Holding tightly to one another they rolled over and over and out of the tent onto the cool grass under the ceiling of shining moon and stars. They went beyond what Roza had ever conceived of before.

They continued to kiss and explore the topography of each other's bodies, leaving shame behind, going beyond fear and anxiety, releasing themselves from the mind, finally giving into the wild pounding of desire and body and breaths that got faster and faster, guiding them to the body's southern hemisphere. They slid on the grass, crushing wild pennyroyals and forget-me-nots, and then, submerged in the clear river, forgot themselves. They let the water cleanse and carry away their memories and pasts. The man plunged wildly into her and she grabbed greedily at his hardened loins. Later, when each of them remembered that wild, rebellious night in the recesses of their hearts, they couldn't recall how many times they climaxed inside each other . . . three times? Ten times? So many times, that when their wet bodies, intertwined like slippery, breathless snakes, awoke at dawn, they could not yet imagine their bodies separating. Again and again, they dipped into one another, plunged in, were released, and allowed the sun to do as it does; become morning, noon, and night. And in the end, they found themselves high upon the enlightenment of love.

CHAPTER 10

There was nobody left to enjoy the newly rebuilt house with five bedrooms, living room, parlour and open kitchen; to sit beside the flames in the large fireplace, drinking tea and flipping through a magazine or reading a book while listening to the joyful sounds of the other family members each busy pursuing their dreams. No! This house was no longer anyone's home . . . Even though the new green velvet furniture accentuated the beauty of the sunset in the parlour. Even though its large library had been refilled with books. Even though the grove with its rows of Japanese quince, yellow jasmine, and purple iris had become so beautiful that the eye never tired of beholding them.

The house was so new that it still smelt of fresh paint, and termites had yet to make their way into any of its wooden recesses. For the first time, the house was equipped with a hot-water heater they could turn on whenever they liked to wash the dishes with warm water, or stay in the shower or the porcelain bathtub as long as their hearts desired, without Mom's constant nagging about the oil running out or worrying that the water would get cold. But alas, was there anyone left? Dad and Granddad's newly framed calligraphy, the antique carpets that had survived the black snow and mice, and the new satin curtains were so pleasant that they left Dad and Beeta feeling sickened in the returned state of mourning. Sickened by all of this beauty, without an owner. Beauty, without a viewer. When Mom left, it was the straw that broke the camel's back for both of them.

That day, in particular, Mom had made the bed and pulled open the curtains so the sun would shine in on the carpet which created a soft reflection of colored light. Then she went to the kitchen to put the kettle on the stove. As he did every morning, Dad had gone to pick fresh flowers from the garden and put them in the new porcelain and crystal vases. While waiting for the water to boil, Mom went into the parlor that had just been decorated with green furniture and curtains and on whose walls hung, at Dad's insistence, pictures of their ancestors. Without opening the curtains, she sat down in an armchair facing the garden and watched Dad through the glass door as he cut roses with his gardening shears and whistled Banan's 'Caravan'. How peaceful and beautiful and fresh everything had become under the caress of the soft light raining into the room through the green curtains. The grove, the house, and Razan had escaped the scourge of death. It seemed that one could continue living, as though it was possible to not think about Bahar and Sohrab, but accept the fact of their deaths. As Mom sat watching Dad through the door, she thought she might just decide to finally break the spell of sorrow that had been cast over the house and laugh out loud. After all, despite everything, life goes on. The sun was still shining, Dad and Beeta were here, and through everything, the moonlit nights were so poetic and beautiful that she wanted to sink into Hushang's masculine embrace and listen to his ragged voice singing, *O sweet Elahe,/ O join in my heart's emotions.*

A faint smile crept over her lips as she thought of Sohrab's poem:

Last night somebody died
and still, wheat bread is good
and water flows down, horses drink.

Just as Dad moved from the garden in front of the house to

the garden in the back, to cut some yellow roses, Mom got up from the green velvet armchair with the carved wooden arm-rests, crossed the parlor's pale green, handwoven carpet, entered the living room, and from there went out onto the porch. She calmly descended the seven steps to the mosaicked courtyard, and from there put her foot on the first of one-hun-dred-and-seventy-five steps that led to the grove and were lined with Japanese quince, yellow jasmine, Spanish broom, and ver-bena. At the bottom of the steps, as her toes felt the moisture of the morning dew on the clovers, saxifrage, and grass, she felt her mind slowly emptying of names and of the thoughts that just minutes before had made her happy. She tried to think of something, anything. But as soon as she stepped through the grove's iron gate and onto the dirt path leading to the village, her mind suddenly stopped. It became silent. Empty. As she crossed the village square and the people looked at her in con-fusion she realized she could no longer even think about the hollowness of her mind. All she could do was go.

It was thus that when Dad entered the house with his bou-quet of red, yellow, and white roses and heard the splashing of water boiling over onto the gas burner, his heart flooded with sudden fear. He turned off the flame on the stove, put the flow-ers on the new kitchen counter and went to the bedroom to find Mom; then checked the other rooms. He woke Beeta up to ask if she knew where Mom was. Then he went out onto the porch and called her name—which he had always thought was the most poetic in the world—over and over again: "Roza! . . . Roza! . . . Roza!"

That bouquet of flowers was never arranged in any vase; it wilted there on the kitchen counter. Even Beeta, until the day she left the house, wouldn't allow herself to touch those dry stalks and petals that would disintegrate to dust and mix with the air at the slightest touch. Dad continued to call Mom's name from time to time, and didn't get up from the porch chair for three days. When he did, his hair had gone completely white. White as snow. Just like Mom's hair after the enlightenment of the greengage tree.

Dad stopped gardening and making frames. The only thing he could do was sit in the rocking chair on the porch where once he sat with Sohrab and Mom and Beeta; but now he listened to the silence of nature, broken occasionally by a distant cooing or mooing of a cow. Months went by, and though I visited them every day, neither Dad nor Beeta were recognizable. Beeta didn't even take the time any more to think about her forgotten dreams, or wipe the dust off her pink ballet slippers that, by now, had become much too small for her. She had to fill everyone's role herself. She cooked. She cleaned the house. She spoke of books. She put cassettes of Marzieh or Banan on in the stereo. She gardened and recited poetry, aloud:

Sometimes that
which leads to truth
itself lacks
as only truth
sets us free.
It is our fate
perhaps
that which we want
either we do not get
or it escapes us.[27]

She washed the dishes and sang, all the while talking of plans she knew would never come to pass. She felt she had no

[27] From "Geh Deinen Weg" by the German poet, Margot Bickel, translated from a translation into Persian by Ahmad Shamlou.

other choice but to talk constantly, because the silence was so heavy it could easily shake the foundation of that strong, new house and bring it down on both of them.

Finally, one morning on an ordinary day while Beeta was washing the dishes and looking out from the kitchen at the tall grass in the grove, the unpruned trees, and untended soil, she thought it would be good to bring some life to the grove now that it was emptied of family members. It was thus that she went to the village to hire a gardener. Everyone pointed to Issa's house. He was perhaps the only young man of the village who had escaped the war and could manage the five-hectare grove on his own. When Beeta crossed the village square and reached the path that led to Issa's house, she didn't know that she would soon be entering a house that, even though it had been years since anyone had knocked on its door, stories of what had happened there were still told by all the villagers, which neither the Revolution nor the war, the forced recruitment of soldiers nor the martyrdom of the young men, the black snow nor the transfiguration of the orphan mothers, could wipe from their memory.

The fate of some is infused with death as simply as the fate of others is with wealth, poverty, or disease. Issa doesn't have a mother. She died giving birth to him. Issa doesn't have a father either. His father followed the First Soothsayer into Razan's fire and burned. Nor does Issa have a sister. His sister, Effat, who came to my treehouse and sought to sweeten some of the village's bitter memories by showing me the treasure had, with one glance, contracted black love for a shepherd boy passing through Razan with a hundred head of sheep, and had died for the love of him.

Issa's mother, Razan and all the distant forest dwellers' only midwife, died giving birth to Issa because she had broken a promise given years before to the forest jinns. Razan's younger generation might call it superstition, but the older people had seen the whole thing with their own eyes and believed in it as they did the sun rising every day in the east. From childhood, Issa's mother, Parvaneh, had healing and midwifery power that she had received from the jinns because one day Parvaneh's mother, Homeyra Khatun, saw a young jinn in her courtyard drinking water from the well. The young jinn looked just like a human except her feet were hoofed, her body was covered with hair, and she was so dirty that she gave off a putrid stench of death that could be smelt from several meters away. Homeyra Khatun immediately used the nail she had in her hand to nail the young jinn's skirt to the ground, and the young jinn who was terrified of iron just like all of her kind, wouldn't even touch it. So that the very same day, Homeyra Khatun bathed her, removed the nits and lice from her hair, dressed her in clean clothes and nailed horse shoes to her feet. From that day forward, the jinn, who in the house was called Jinni, became a servant and cook for Homeyra Khatun who, finding herself alone to raise six sons and one daughter, had to take care of the house as well as work in the rice paddies.

Homeyra Khatun knew that Jinni's mother was looking for her, so she didn't allow her out into the courtyard. The young jinn's mother spent years looking for her daughter—going from grove to grove, from courtyard to courtyard, from bath-house to bathhouse, until one ordinary summer afternoon on one of many ordinary days, she caught sight of her daughter removing the ashes from the cooking stove as she was passing by Homeyra Khatun's basement. Jinni's mother sat down right then and there and sobbed. Later, she went to the forest jinns to discuss how best to rescue her daughter from the humans. One of them came up with a plan: it was thus that Homeyra Khatun's headaches began. At first Homeyra Khatun thought the headaches were due to heat exhaustion and excessive work in the paddies. But then when her headaches got worse by the day, not letting up for even a minute, they brought in the First Soothsayer. "What are your headaches like?" he asked. "It feels as if someone keeps hitting me over the head with a copper dustpan," Homeyra Khatun replied. The Soothsayer recited some incantations and, as soon as he had placed the mirror in front of Homeyra Khatun, he saw a jinn hitting her over the head with a copper dustpan. As the Soothsayer waved incense, he told Homeyra Khatun what he had seen. Before leaving, he stared at the jinn in the mirror and tried some common de-jinning methods. But in the end, he said, "The charm they put on you can only be broken by you, yourself." And so in the middle of that very night, Homeyra Khatun took Jinni out into the courtyard and began to sweep. As soon as the jinn mother heard the *frrrt . . . frrrt . . . frrrt* of the broom, she had no choice but to appear and say loudly, "So you know all our tricks! I wanted to come and bargain with you for the return of my daughter. But now it appears you have summoned me and that *you* want to do the bargaining." Homeyra Khatun quickly got to the point, saying, "If you want your daughter back, you have to give seven generations of my family's daughters healing powers." When the jinn heard this, she said to the woman, "Open your mouth." The woman opened her mouth, whereupon the jinn spat inside and said, "From now on, seven generations of your daughters and your daughter's daughters will be able to heal with their saliva." Then she added, "Now your side of the deal." But Homeyra Khatun did not keep her promise, instead saying, "I have one more condition. My condition is that seven generations of my daughters must be the best midwives of Razan and all the surrounding forested area so they become wealthy and more powerful than their husbands."

The jinn had no choice but to say, "Give me your hands." The woman stretched out her hands and once again the jinn spat, this time on her hands, saying, "Here. From now on seven generations of your daughters will be the best midwives in the region and they will be swimming in wealth." At this, Homeyra Khatun removed the horseshoes from the young girl's hooves with a wrench. As soon as the mother had taken her daughter's hand in her own, the jinn said, "But since you didn't keep your promise, mark my words: from this moment forward I will be your enemy and the enemy of seven generations of your family. If you tell your daughter of their powers, the charm will be broken. They must discover their powers on their own." Then she pulled down her stinky hemp breeches and peed into the well. Unable to do anything, Homeyra Khatun just stood there looking at the jinn whose urine was flowing into the water. Whereupon, in the blink of an eye, the jinn and her daughter disappeared.

From that day and for seven generations until now, no one touched the well water. It increased so much every year that it overflowed into the courtyard, the garden, and then the grove, bewitching and poisoning all the plants. It was thus that the jinn's first act of enmity towards the family became problematic. However, it wasn't long before Parvaneh, Homeyra Khatun's only daughter, discovered that her touch not only relieved the pain caused by the villagers' rotten teeth so she could pull them out without inflicting pain, but she could also cure, forever, the aches felt in the crooked, damp joints of old men and women. She wasn't yet the talk of the town when she discovered she could painlessly deliver the babies of expecting mothers; even though she was young enough to still wet her bed at night and hugged her cloth doll to her chest to fall asleep, her fame soon spread from the village to the surrounding villages and the forested area beyond.

She had not yet turned eleven when she assisted her hundredth birth. Homeyra Khatun, whose wish for wealth had come true, wanted to make a votive offering of food to distribute to the people. But that very evening, a jinn came into Parvaneh's room. Parvaneh, who had heard stories of forest jinns from her mother and grandmother, recognized her immediately and said, "What is it you want with me?" The jinn answered, "Respect for tradition! For every hundred human births, you must also assist one of ours." Before Parvaneh could answer, she saw herself passing through the wall of her house, through the roof, and flying over the forest, pulled along by the jinn who had taken her arm and was leading the way. When they finally landed on the forest floor under a dense canopy of trees, the jinn snapped her fingers. In the blink of an eye, what had previously been as dark as death and terrifying was illuminated with dozens of candles and torches. Parvaneh saw dozens of jinns, small and large, with ugly black faces, matted hair, and hoof-like feet all doing something. One was spinning invisible thread, another was leaning against a tree memorizing ancient incantations from an invisible notebook. One was writing a vagabondage jinx with urine from a baby jinn, and yet another was preparing food in a large pot, the stench of which made Parvaneh's stomach turn. Lying on the ground in the middle of all of this was a jinn, screaming with labor pains. Parvaneh, who all the time had been telling herself she wouldn't help the jinns, suddenly took mercy. She stepped forward and, as soon as she had placed a hand on the pregnant jinn's stomach, the baby was born without any pain. Nearby, Jinni's mother recognized Parvaneh and her miraculous touch, and recalled her oath to Homeyra Khatun, but said nothing. When the job was done and she had returned home, the jinn placed several onion skins under the corner of the rug in Parvaneh's room and said, "This is your payment. If you keep this a secret and tell no one, in the morning you will find a gold coin under the rug. However, if you say anything to anyone, not only will you be severely punished, but you will be left nothing but onion skins." No sooner had the jinn spoken these words than she disappeared.

For years, things continued accordingly and, before falling in love, Parvaneh owned ten hectares of rice paddies, twenty hectares of groves, hundreds of hens, roosters, ducks, and geese, and a vat full of gold coins, the provenance of which nobody, not even her mother, was aware. When Parvaneh was only sixteen years old, she fell in love with Qorban, son of the village leader. Their wedding celebration lasted seven days and seven nights. Less than a year after the birth of their daughter Effat, Qorban was awoken in the middle of the night by a nightmare. He had dreamed that his wife had died giving birth to a son. He reached out in the dark towards Parvaneh but found no trace of her. He became even more frightened. The more he searched, the less he found. It seemed as if she had disappeared into thin air. It was almost dawn when, after having dozed off for several minutes out of fatigue and anger, Qorban awoke to find Parvaneh sleeping in her usual place. He was seething with jealousy. That very morning, he grabbed several gold coins and went to see the Soothsayer, and told him what had happened. The Soothsayer looked into the mirror and explained everything. Then he said, "Keep count of the births Effat delivers. After the hundredth delivery, you can expect a jinn to appear. That night sprinkle sawdust on the floor after your wife has gone to sleep. The sawdust will stick to her skirt, and through my powers, will light up like the Milky Way so that you will be able to find her. But you must remember, no matter what happens you must not reveal yourself."

Weeks and months went by until one night when the jinn returned. Taking Parvaneh's hand, she led her up into the sky, with Qorban following, running until he reached the middle of the forest. He hid behind a tree and was watching the birth ritual with amazement when suddenly he was shoved into the midst of the jinns. Everyone screamed. They cursed in an incomprehensible language and, in the blink of an eye, disappeared. When Parvaneh saw him, she fainted out of fear. And so it was that Jinni's mother managed to take her revenge on Homeyra Khatun, for she knew how the fate of every member of that family would change as a result of the mere pressure of her hand on Qorban's back.

When Parvaneh re-awoke, she saw no sign of the jinns. The two of them groped blindly in the dark towards their house, while Parvaneh cursed Qorban in her heart for his stupidity and meddling, all the while expecting a mysterious death to strike at any moment. From that night on, and every night before going to sleep, Parvaneh told Qorban to take good care of Effat if the jinns took her life and she didn't live till morning.

It was the first sign, but the most important one: Parvaneh's left arm began to itch, and didn't stop until the day she died. When the itching in her left arm didn't even let up as she slept, she knew she would soon lose her wealth. The second sign revealed the limits of her physical reality; she lost her miraculous touch. Now she had two hands just like everyone else and saliva that couldn't even cure bloating in a cow or diarrhea in a mule. By the time the third sign appeared, she was so worried and frightened that she had lost ten kilos and had taken up praying again, something she had given up at the age of ten. One night, an unknown fever hit the chickens, and before dawn the inhabitants of Razan were awoken by the smell of their carcasses. That foggy morning when Parvaneh stepped on the ducks' putrid bodies, poured petrol over them, and set fire to them, she knew what it all meant. In the thick fog, away from the noise of the flames that were spreading the smell of burnt wood and roasting meat in all directions, she sat down and thought, *this is just the beginning*. It wasn't long before her citrus trees and rice paddies were attacked by parasites, which destroyed the whole harvest but didn't even touch neighboring land. When this happened Qorban consoled himself by saying, "Let them take all we own." But even when Parvaneh fell pregnant upon the advice of her mother, Homeyra Khatun, so that with the birth of a daughter she might rid herself of the malevolence and curse of what had happened and ensure another generation of healer-midwives, Parvaneh wasn't so calm. So, when one early morning nine months later, Issa opened his eyes to the world, his mother Parvaneh, without as much as a meter of land to her name, closed her own eyes forever, and Qorban was to spend years, thereafter, searching for her vat of gold coins; the very vat he found, years later, filled with onion skins in the poisoned well. With Parvaneh's death and the birth of a son, Homeyra Khatun hoped that at least Effat would continue her path, win the jinns over again, and regain all the riches and property that had been lost. However, these hopes were dashed years later with Effat's self-immolation. Stricken by black love, Effat set herself on fire before discovering she had powers of healing and midwifery.

Beeta, who knew nothing of these events, heard an unfamiliar sound coming from the other side of the wooden door as she knocked; a sound like a slithering or scraping on the ground. It was the crazed slithering and scraping of the jinxed plants and flowers in Homeyra Khatun's garden, which in recent months had turned Issa mad and enchanted him. In recent months, with his mind at a standstill in mourning for his father, mother, and sister, Issa had sat staring at the growing plants, and he remained prisoner of that nameless mania until the day Beeta came knocking. Issa and Homeyra Khatun— who was now so old she couldn't even remember her own name—still lived in the house with the well jinxed by jinn urine. Although Dad and the other villagers had wanted to rebuild her house after the black snow, Homeyra Khatun had insistently refused to budge, not even allowing them to enter the courtyard. Now the shabby and collapsing adobe house, forcibly propped up and besieged by thorns, weeds, and slimy mosses growing and sticking to everything fed by the well water, was struggling to breathe as it was swallowed whole. It was Homeyra Khatun's destiny to witness her daughter's death and to have nothing but a burial shroud to her name when she herself passed away.

When the well was jinxed, the family's task had become cutting back the plants that enveloped the walls, windows, courtyard, and roof in their constant creeping and scraping. However, with the death first of Parvaneh, then Effat, and finally Qorban, Issa's motivation decreased daily until recently, he no longer even laid a finger on the sickle. Now, he just sat and watched the insufferable crackling of the plants, the flowers, and the trees as they grew, and crept, and pulled themselves over the ground; sprouting, flowering, and bearing fruit right before his eyes. Fruits that, in all these years, neither he nor anyone else had ever eaten.

The inhabitants of Razan soon realized that Issa had contracted an unknown mania. A mania that was so new it had yet to be given a name. A manic addiction to the agonizing sounds of the plants creeping and grating as they grew obstinately, insatiably; just to prove how easily they could violate the laws of nature within the confines of that small courtyard.

Once, not long before, as Issa sat on the porch where, until recently, Effat would sit combing her long hair with a wooden comb, he closed his eyes and heard how the honeysuckle vines slithered over from the garden to the courtyard, crept up the porch steps and then wrapped around his ankle, moving upward until they reached his back, arms, and neck. If Homeyra Khatun hadn't arrived in time with the weed killer she had made out of some plants, petrol, salt, and lime, within hours Issa would have become a dried-up tree, and the vines, like ivy, would have driven their roots into his body, and eventually honeysuckle blossoms would have sprouted from his ears, mouth, and nose.

The sound followed him everywhere; with windows open or closed; whether he sealed the cracks around the doors and windows with wax or not. This endless slithering, creeping, devouring sound was killing him. There was nothing anyone could do; not Homeyra Khatun, not the Soothsayer, until Beeta, unaware of all the madness that had come to pass in that village house, knocked several times and was about to give up when Issa eventually opened the door. A tall young man with miserable, bashful, honey-colored eyes hidden under long, light brown hair, stood before her. Beeta got right to the point and Issa, without giving it a moment's thought and without saying a word, nodded his head in agreement and closed the door again. From that moment on Issa became Beeta's employee. He became the gardener of a five-hectare grove, with the ability to interpret dragonflies.

The next morning at dawn, as the dewdrops were slowly evaporating and rising like sleeping spirits from the earth into the air, and the dragonflies were sunning themselves in the sun's hot rays, Beeta saw Issa, sickle in hand, cutting back the grove's long grass and weeds. After a week like this Beeta felt that, contrary to her hopes, Issa had not brought life to the grove, but seemed to have added to its heaviness and silence, and sorrow. It was thus that she told him to hire five more workers to weed under the citrus trees, loosen the soil and spread fertilizer. A day later, Beeta and Hushang awoke to the commotion of the new gardeners, three of whom were women. Happy with all the noise, Beeta went out onto the porch and thought, *Women always bring passion and life*. And yet, Hushang's behaviour did not change. He still did absolutely nothing. He didn't help with the housework or even read a book, or make a picture frame. He still just sat on the porch looking at Razan and the bustle of new life in the grove.

Beeta gladly prepared food and tea for all six of the workers and spent hours with them every day. She spoke with them.
She learned how to use the sickle as skillfully as they did, how
to use a hatchet and how to weed. She joined in the girls' con-
versations and meddled in their fates. She tried to rid herself of
me as much as possible—as I was nothing more than a ghost—
and Dad, who had become nothing but a moving corpse. She
wanted to rid herself of thoughts of Mom and Sohrab and even
force some excitement into her daily life. She wanted to be
alive and interact with the living. It was thus that one day she
startled Issa putting her hand on his arm as he was pruning a
tree. Beeta had wanted to comfort Issa, as I had recently told
her about his mother. However, the pressure of her touch upon
his arm, and perhaps also the long look she gave him as she
peered into his honey-colored eyes seemed to be more than he
could manage, for Issa trembled, flushed, dropped his clippers, and promptly left.

This simple action was the blow that crushed my poor sister. After several days with no sign of Issa or news of him from
the other workers, she contracted a fever and, delirious, realized that she was "stricken." That is, she had fallen in love.
There was no need for her to tell me. She knew that I knew
everything, which perhaps angered her even more. In her first
imperfect and hollow experience of this feeling that bore no
resemblance to the classical love stories she had read, she
wanted to suffer and berate herself in secretive solitude. She
tossed and turned in her hot bed, thinking how foolish she was
to lose herself to a village boy at least five years her junior. She
took a spoonful of soup from the bowl on her bedside table
and promised herself she would get up and stop being so child-
ish as soon as she'd finished the bowl. But the warmth of the
soup hadn't even made it down her throat when her spoon was
refilled by a hot tear. She scolded herself for touching Issa's
arm, and thought this unfamiliar feeling which, like a drop of

ink in water, was growing bigger and bigger by the second, and was about to drown her like an inner morass, should have stayed hidden inside her, forever. Contemptuously she thought, *Love doesn't begin like this. Love isn't even possible without knowing someone, and who said I was in love anyway?* Then for a moment she hated herself because she'd come to the conclusion that her feelings were those of desire. When she was honest with herself, she thought, *Yes, I have to admit that whatever this is, it isn't love. It's nothing but dirty, fleeting, foolish lust; exactly what all the poets and writers say must be distinguished from real love.* Filled with disgust, she reluctantly touched the sticky discharge from her vagina. She hated herself and rebuked herself for not having become more mature given all of life's suffering and her constant reading. Her body was turning her into a person she didn't want to be. It felt like another's body, and she didn't know what to do. She was embarrassed; she realized that at the age of thirty she was only just nearing physical maturity. After that, she began playing with herself in bed. For the first time in her life she allowed herself to respond to her body's natural desires. She locked her bedroom door, put a cassette of Richard Clayderman's piano albums in the stereo, and, fantasizing about Issa's fine hands and tanned face, she touched herself. With unprecedented, unabashed excitement, she removed her clothing piece by piece and let the coolness of the sheets caress her body. She writhed, kissed, and bit her naked shoulders and arms, and when, for the first time in her thirty years she climaxed, it was so intense that she tore her pillow with her teeth, to stifle her cry. Her whole body was covered with sweat and pulsing, and if her orgasm had lasted any longer she thought she probably would've had a heart attack and died, one hand between her legs and the other clutching her firm breast. Afterwards, her whole body felt light, as though a heavy weight had been lifted from her shoulders, as though she had spent several hours in the bathroom with one person scrubbing all the dirt off her body, another massaging her, and a third caressing her with gentle hands to make her calm and supple. Her first orgasm left her with a mixture of pleasant emotions and physical sensations she had never known before. She masturbated four more times that night while fantasizing about Issa. The next morning, she awoke with such a sense of guilty joy that she went to the bathroom and vomited. She didn't know why she should hate herself or be ashamed of this one-person pleasure. She didn't know if what she'd done was normal or if she was the only person in the whole world who derived pleasure from touching her own body. As she vomited in the bathroom she realized she couldn't recall a single instance of this with the heroes or heroines of the books she had read or the films she had seen. She thought that even if Mom were around she would never allow herself to ask her about it, much less Dad. And so after bathing, she took refuge in her bed once more and began to re-read all her tales of love and romance. She was looking for signs of how to distinguish real love from false love, or at least to see if in any of those turbulent stories of love anyone ever masturbated!

As the days went on, she found increasing solace in the fact she'd been able to distinguish between love and lust right from the beginning, and hadn't lost her physical or emotional virginity to fleeting passion. Then she searched the whole house and attic until she found and devoured books on the psychology of marriage, love, sex, and dating, taking the tests in *Know Yourself in Love* over and over again until she had finally chosen all the correct answers.

On the seventeenth day, while Beeta was lying on her bed giving the sunlight a smile, a smile whose only meaning could have been, *Thank goodness I survived this chronic plague!*; and just as she was feeling most resistant to physical lust and false love, all resolve was lost with the first "Miss Beeta" she heard coming from Issa's mouth. All the strength of will she had gained from logic, psychological analyses and know-thyself quizzes evaporated as she carried herself on shaky legs to the window to make sure it was, in fact, he who was saying, "Please come to the fire temple. I have to talk to you!" with such confidence and abandon.

Contrary to my expectations, this time it was not Beeta who touched Issa's arm, but rather Issa who caressed Beeta's soft brown hair with his sun-browned hands and, turning her head towards his own, kissed her with a confidence that only village boys have toward city girls. With the first kiss all rigid perceptions, self-imposed morals, and books on the psychology of love and self-awareness were set alight, burning the grass, turning to smoke, and vanishing. They took such decisive and imperious possession of one another's physical topography among the trees' intertwined branches, tall bracken, and elderberry stalks, that no words were wasted. It was thus that during the one year, eight months, and two weeks that they made love every day and every night, in body and in soul, neither of them took the time to say, "I love you," or ask, "Do you love me?" Issa bent over Beeta's delicate, downtrodden frame with his athletic village build and pressed himself against her with such force it seemed as if he didn't want even a second's separation from her, not so it was. He rarely spoke during lovemaking, and if he did it was to say, "I want to plunge inside you and never come out." Every time they made love the heat generated as they twisted together was so intense the grass around them caught fire and burned. Although the workers were surprised every day when they saw fresh circles of scorched earth, they attributed it to the abnormally hot summer and autumn. Beeta, meanwhile, was still unsure whether or not this disaster that had befallen her was really love. She wondered if humans were capable of falling in love with anyone who makes them happy, and although Issa was a sad, solitary person, he filled her with joy. After the burning of Dad's *tars*, Bahar's death by fire, the book burning, Sohrab's execution, and Mom's leaving, what other reason for joy did she have? She thought the moments of making love with Issa were reminders that life could still be lovely and beautiful despite all the shitty things it dished out. It was still possible to lie in the fresh grass after making clandestine love, smile, and roll a cigarette out of wild grasses and blow its smoke at the butterflies and dragonflies as they watched the fat playful white clouds overhead. Naked, she rolled for long minutes in the grass, letting quiet seconds stretch and ladybirds play in her hair and tickle the tips of her toes. She let joy slowly rejuvenate her body and calm her youth. And she thought about Issa and how wonderful it was that he could interpret dragonflies. Although Issa mostly responded to Beeta's talkativeness or questions with silence, or simply gave an affirmative smile and nodded his head, he hadn't been able to hide his ability to interpret dragonflies.

Years of endless creeping plant tendrils, which twisted and wound together like snakes, kissed the trees' hands and feet, and blossomed from the small nodes at their ends, had turned Issa's courtyard into the perfect haven for beasts and insects; and years of staring at that enchanted garden had given him the opportunity to observe dragonfly movements to such an extent that he had become the only ever dragonfly reader.

When they were together, Issa was always distracted by dragonflies. While he was talking to Beeta or listening to her, his eyes would dart from side to side following their flight. Based on their type, color, where they flew, how they flew, and where they landed, he predicted the day's or week's events. That was the reason he had trembled, dropped his clippers, and fled the day that Beeta had placed a hand on his arm; for at the very moment he had noticed a red dragonfly sitting on Beeta's shoulder. Realizing that an inevitable fiery love was in store for him, he panicked and fled; and the day he saw a yellow dragonfly on his windowpane, he knew the time had come to express his love for her, and not fight it. The first time they made love it was in the presence of a congress of multicolored dragonflies who sat around them on flowers, bushes, and trees, giving him the courage to wholeheartedly enter a romance that he would not easily be able to leave. The dragonflies that burned in their rings of fire each time they made love turned to ash together with the grass and dandelions.

Issa knew if dragonflies hung under a tree branch or the frame of a door, or window, it would soon rain. He knew if they sat on top of a twig that rain would not come; if the first dragonfly to hover around him in the morning was dark, the weather that day would be stormy and there would be thunder and lightning; and if it was multi-colored, a baby would be born in his neighborhood.

Issa told Beeta to be careful not to let a white dragonfly into her room because it signified someone close to her would soon die. But when he saw the ensuing look of sorrow that spread across her face, to erase the effect of that inauspicious statement, he announced, "And if, one day, a green dragonfly lands on your bed, come and tell me quickly, because that is the sign that the time of your marriage will have arrived." And then, both smiling at the thought of the realization of their secret wishes, they smothered one another's bare shoulders in kisses. But a green dragonfly never did land on Beeta's bed, or even flutter around any part of her room, for that matter. Instead, a small blue one landed on Beeta's head one day. Upon seeing it Issa blanched, but no matter how many times she asked him what it meant he wouldn't answer. Rather, he smothered her passionately in kisses as if to bid her farewell.

Just as unexpectedly as Beeta's romance had begun, like a half-completed dream, it ended, torn apart in airy wisps. The day after the blue dragonfly had landed in her hair, Delbar, a village girl with light brown eyes, perky white breasts, and golden hair upon which a green dragonfly was perched, suddenly appeared in front of Issa, giving meaning to Beeta's blue dragonfly. Paying no notice to Issa, Delbar walked past him and continued on her way. But Issa understood immediately that, like it or not, the green dragonfly on her golden hair had signaled the beginning of a new chapter in his life. All his and Beeta's secret lovemaking beside the Zoroastrian fire temple, their furtive meals, their clandestine dressing and undressing, their kisses in the rings of fire, Beeta's beautiful poetic verses that Issa sometimes didn't even understand, all came to an end when the blue dragonfly landed on Beeta's head, and Issa knew he had to respect the laws of nature. So, he turned around and inspected Delbar's appealing physique. Standing there dumbstruck by the green dragonfly flitting around her head, he forgot that at that very moment Beeta was waiting in their spot beside the fire temple to caress his straight brown hair and whisper in his ear, "See what I've got myself into? . . . See how I've been stricken by you?" And although Issa had never understood what she meant, he never asked, "What does 'stricken' mean?"

That day, Beeta sat beside the fire temple looking at the circles of scorched earth until dark. Each ring bore the memory of one or even multiple love-makings. In some parts of the yard the burnt circles were sprinkled with grass, while in others they were so scorched there was no hope that fresh blades would sprout. She wore a satisfied smile, but as the minutes passed and still Issa didn't appear, while several colorless dragonflies flew and landed on either side of her, as if they were his messengers, the circles became menacing. Gradually she began hearing a buzzing in her head and then, as though preparing itself for something ominous, her mind stood still, and she saw time pause and all movement cease. During this pause, two ladybirds and three dragonflies landed on wild dog-rose bushes around her and then left, a baby fox peeked out from the bracken and elderberry and fled when it saw her, and the crickets didn't stop chirping. She didn't see any of this, though. Her eyes were open, yet she couldn't see. Issa still hadn't come. She had to do something. She blinked, but still she was blind. The crickets continued chirping and still she was blind. She thought, *What an astonishingly sudden blindness*. Yet she didn't move. She was frightened, but didn't show it. She touched a blade of grass with her fingers, picked it, and raised it to her mouth. When her hand reached her lips, she could feel both they and her hands trembling. She strained to see something, at least the scorched patches of earth. But she had stared so long at the black circles that the blackness was expanding, getting larger and larger until it took over her mind. She allowed time to restart. Gradually her static mind recognized that time had slowly, elastically resumed its movement. She felt something move in front of her. She blinked again and made out the head of the fox, which had returned to take another peek. Slowly she saw the blades of grass moving, and the threatening circles took shape.

When the sun finally set and the owls began hooting, and the nightingales and sparrows had gone to sleep, she stood up, walked across the grass past Dad on the porch, and entered her room. She turned on the light. Looking carefully at every part of the room, she confirmed that her eyesight had returned. She pulled out the *I Ching* from among her books, made a wish, and threw three coins six times on the floor, writing down the results on a piece of paper. Six lines.

Exhaustion: A man permits himself to be oppressed by stone and leans on thorns and thistles.
He enters the house and does not see his wife.
Misfortune . . .

Her eyes filled with tears. She took a deep breath and looked out the window at Venus which had just risen. She read on:

> *He is oppressed by creeping vines.*
> *He moves uncertainly and says, "Movement brings remorse."*

It was then that, for the first time, she, herself, interpreted a dragonfly. At least now she knew the reading of the blue dragonfly on her head.

Several days later, the female workers shared the news; but Issa never came to see her, even to say goodbye.

She didn't get a fever. She didn't brood. She didn't even go to fetch her ballet slippers. After a few days, she stopped staring at the scorched circles. She packed some things for herself and Dad in a small bag, and as she was putting on her sneakers she went out to him on the porch and said, "Get up. Get dressed. Let's go to Tehran. There's nothing left for us here."

Dad looked at her as if from very far away, smiled, and said, "I'm staying here."

"In Tehran we can live in Granddad's house," Beeta insisted. "There's room for us there."

Dad replied, "I still have work to do here."

Scornfully Beeta said, "Like what?"

"I don't know yet," Dad said, simply.

Then he kissed Beeta on the cheek and said, "Go to university. Study a subject that you like, and be someone that good people want to meet. Maybe you'll return one day. I'll be waiting for you here until then."

Crying as she left, Beeta descended the hill and with the help of the dragonflies, foot paths, cows, loose horses, and gypsies that occasionally wandered the forests, she hoped to find her way to the main road.

CHAPTER 11

The wind sings of our nostalgia
The star-filled sky ignores our dreams
And each snowflake is like a tear unshed
Silence is full of words unsaid
Actions uncompleted
A confession of secret loves
And marvels unspoken
In this silence our truth is hidden
Yours and mine.[28]

Maybe it never would have come to this if Beeta had taken Issa's silence more seriously. Brokenhearted and hurt by his unfaithfulness, and although she had been unable to plumb Issa's depths over the whole year, eight months, and two weeks that she had been in love with him, Beeta left Razan to forge a new path among the living. Issa's silence had been a gulf between them that was filled with love making.

It wasn't that Issa had sought to hide anything, he just saw his life as so full of fate, anguish, and despair that he had become accustomed to keeping silent. He had become accustomed to keeping silent about the jinns' enchantments and his grandmother's conniving; the plants' maniacal growth in the courtyard, Effat's black love, Razan's sacred fire, and his

[28] By Margot Bickel, translated from a Persian translation by Ahmad Shamlou.

father's transfiguration. And yet, perhaps if Beeta had really wanted and had made a real effort to be part of Issa's life, she could have heard many stories from the people or even me. Perhaps if she had wanted to take their relationship beyond those rings of fire, closer to real life, she could have searched for the meaning of Issa's long silences instead of striving to interpret dragonflies.

People still say many things about Issa's family, especially about his sister. People say that the mouth and body of someone stricken by black love gives off a fragrance contagious to anyone who comes near and smells it, even if they are not in love. Even if they are old. Even if they are children. They fall in love, become infatuated, obsessed. Effat was stricken by black love the day that a young shepherd passing through Razan, for the first and last time, happened to ask Effat, who was sitting on her porch spinning thread, for a sip of water before leaving. Effat gave him water in a blue ceramic cup she had made herself and, just as the young boy bent his head to drink from it she caught sight of the undulant, shining reflection of his face in the water, and promptly fell in love. She became stricken, feverish, captured. It was as simple as that.

Someone stricken by black love stops speaking. Or, if they speak, they speak only of love. They rarely work, but when they do, they work feverishly, until they collapse from exhaustion. Effat became obsessed with going for walks on moonlit nights. Her long hair brushed, she would set off, barefoot, as soon as the sun went down. Her steps were sure and steady, but aimless. From grove to grove. From meadow to meadow. From courtyard to courtyard, and from stable to stable. In the beginning her father and Issa, her only brother, would go looking for her and find her in a neighbor's stable, a meadow in the depths of the forest, or in a distant rice paddy, sitting in the moonlight combing her hair with her wooden comb and quietly singing love songs. The last time that Qorban and Issa had set off after her in the dark, they found her in a meadow several villages over, crawling on all fours, eating grass, and bleating. She was ripping the grass up from beneath the snow with her teeth and chewing it. On that cold moonlit winter night, the meadow was covered with snow, and the moon's silvery reflection had multiplied the snow's illusions; every twig and branch loomed larger, tempting those who passed to go towards the elastic shadows, to touch them, take them. But Qorban had warned Issa not to be tricked by the shadows. He had told him, "Just follow me, cover your ears, and don't look around. Every shadow on a snowy, moonlit night could be a jinn, a *nasnas*, a fairy, or a *davalpa*."[29] That night when they reached the large meadow and they heard singing, Qurban stopped and said, "Cover your ears. It's the sound of the fairies, jinns, and *davalpas* who want to seduce us." Issa covered his ears but wondered all the same, why would they want to seduce us? His father brought his mouth close to Issa's ear and said quickly, "Because the fairies and jinns want to breed with us and the *davalpa* wants us to toil for him." Issa couldn't understand why fairies and jinns would want such a thing but there was no more time for questions. Walking with their ears covered, the sound came nearer and nearer until the father heard the bleating. They approached cautiously. Qorban signalled to Issa to stay where he was. His father moved towards the creature, until gradually he made out his daughter; Effat's head was lowered, and she was ripping frozen grass from under the snow with her teeth. Upon seeing his daughter like this, Qorban felt all the world's

[29] In the Quran and religious stories, *nasnases* are creatures similar to humans but with one leg and one arm, who are said to have been created before man. They are considered to be sinning, transgressing creatures; *davalpas* have the upper body of a man and a lower body of a snake. They sit on the side of the road at night looking for a ride. As soon as they are seated behind someone the *davalpas* wrap their snake-like legs around the person, forcing him to work for them.

sorrow tumble down on him. He sat down next to Effat and said, "My daughter, you are not a sheep." Effat stopped eating grass, and with complete innocence said, "What do you know?" Then she smiled kindly at her father. Her father said, "I was there when you were born. Your mother named you 'Effat'. Your mother was also human." Effat looked at him again and said, "You mean, you still don't understand?" Her father asked, "Understand what?" "That nothing is the reason for all things?" Effat replied with finality.

Effat always smiled. Black love made people kind; kind and sad. That night, Qorban and Issa finally convinced Effat to come back to the house with them. Like all the villagers, Qorban knew that the consequence of black love would be death. There was no other cure. He couldn't just sit and do nothing, however. He tried different things. He took her to the shrine on the mountain and gave her to the caretaker there, but a week later they saw her sitting on the steps of the *tekyeh* with torn clothes talking to the shadows in the middle of the night. The people saw her turn to the shadows and say, "*baaaaaaaaa . . . baaaaaaaa . . .* I am your sheep . . . I am your servant . . . just come back once and pass through this village . . . See how beautifully I am bleating for you . . . *baaaaaaaaa . . . baaaaaaaa . . .*" Then she cried, stood up, mounted the wooden steps of the *tekyeh*, and rubbed her hand along the carved wood *saqa nefar* as she pleaded and cried. She wiped her tears away with her long hair, looked up to the sky and said, "You left your little darling lamb here . . . Won't you come back and take her with you? Your innocent little lamb is wasting away all alone . . . Come and take me, kill me, and take my flesh as your food . . . may it nourish you. *Baaaaaaaaaaaa . . . baaaaaaaaaaaa.* Have you forgotten how you carried me under your arm and played the flute for me in the deserts and on the plains?" Then the distraught woman began to sob once more and said, "See? I am without owner . . . no matter how much I bleat nobody comes to take me to their stable . . . for everyone knows that I am your little, lost, white lamb . . . *baaaaaaaa baaaaaaa.*"

Several days later, when Qorban was out and Effat was sitting as always on the edge of the porch combing her hair with a wooden comb and watching the steady snowfall, Issa finally worked up the courage to come and sit beside her. He started sniffing the air. Aside from the smell of cold snow, he couldn't smell anything. He edged closer and sniffed again. This time he detected a scent that wasn't snow. He sat even closer, their bodies touching. In the dead of winter the warmth of Effat's body was like an oven. He stuck his nose in Effat's hair and sniffed. Suddenly a wild fragrance took possession of him. It was a fragrance like none other he had known. He became dizzy and felt that if it continued much longer he would never be able to free himself from it. Moving away from her in a panic, he sat in the courtyard directly under the falling snow. The wild fragrance of Effat's body would not leave him, however. His nerves were shattered; he wanted to pounce on Effat again, on her body and hair. But as he hastened back to her, he turned around midway and, frightened, went out of the courtyard and didn't come back until that night. Issa's reaction was not lost on Effat who, smiling, finally lifted her head and watched him walk away under the heavy snow. She whispered to herself, "Oh poor thing. You don't understand it, either," and continued combing her hair.

The next morning, Issa was still thinking of just one thing: the people were right, the smell drives you mad. He wanted to stay in the house all day so he wouldn't have to pass by Effat and smell that irresistible scent. However, without knowing how it happened, he found himself several seconds later sitting next to her once more. He asked, "Are you really in love?" Effat looked at him with surprise and said, "What does 'in love' mean?" Issa said, "You know, it's what people say when they have a crush on someone."

"How can a leaf have a crush on a tree? Is that even possible? Can a lamb have a crush on his shepherd? Do 'shepherd' and 'tree' mean anything without 'lamb' and 'leaf'? Confused, Issa asked, "What are you trying to say?" "One day I saw someone who stood with me for a few minutes and asked for a cup of water, drank it, and then left. And I realized I had suddenly become two. That's it. Since that day, I've been two. Do you understand?" Effat said. Issa didn't understand. Effat shook her head, then suddenly said angrily, "You're all crazy. None of you understands what it means to be two. All of you are so stuck on your one self that you don't even understand why you are alive!" Then she calmly returned to combing her hair. It blew in the gentle breeze. She laughed and said, "My only problem is that my two are separated. I need to fix that, that's all." "Where is your other one now?" he asked. Effat stopped combing, stared at an indistinct point in the air, and said, "Standing under a lone tree facing a meadow and looking at his flock scattered over the plain." She paused and then speaking again said, "Just now he bent down and is drinking cool water from the spring at his feet." Closing her eyes to feel the refreshing coolness of the water in every cell of her body— she really had been thirsty—she took a deep breath again and said, "How cool it is! Would you like some?" Ignoring her offer, Issa said, "Where are you going next?"

"To winter pastures with the Charva tribe. We're going toward the Kalimani plains," she replied, enigmatically.

The next day, the Soothsayer came to their house with some elders. The elders were thankful since the presence of the Soothsayer protected them from Effat's fragrant breath so that nothing could happen to them. There was no need for the old man to open his book to recognise that the girl had been enchanted. "Black magic." The elders asked what they should do. The Soothsayer said, "Bring me a bowl of water." Then, turning towards the village leader he said, "Send someone to bring some urine from your newborn grandson." They called a boy and gave him the message. The boy ran off and returned an hour later with a small ceramic bowl of urine from the young male child. The Soothsayer poured the urine into the bowl of water. He said, "Bring a fresh piece of cloth."

When they brought it, he put his hands under the cloth and asked the village's only Haji to hold the mirror above his hands. Calling Effat over to sit in front of him, the Soothsayer took her hands and put them in the bowl of urine under the cloth. Suddenly the cloth began to move. The bowl beneath it was rattling. Bubbling. Drops of urine sprayed left and right like hot coals, burning the felt rugs on which the villagers were standing. Creatures were forming inside the cloth and had begun to move around. Pouring sweat, the Soothsayer was trying to keep those squirming creatures under the cloth when suddenly, all became still and silent. Silent. Silent.

The villagers stood there, frozen. They were holding their breath. The only one who was laughing with an innocent kindness was Effat. The Soothsayer's eyes had been closed. He now opened them and looked at Effat, who was smiling as if nothing had happened. The Soothsayer threw the cloth into a corner and the wide-eyed, frightened villagers saw that the bowl of urine now contained dirt and padlocks, jinxes and black magic. Effat looked at the locks and laughed. The Soothsayer asked, "Do you know how they had locked your fortune, girl? These are locks of your fate that the jinns brought to me from under the earth." Then he pulled out some frankincense, fragrant wood, and an incense burner from his bag. Once he had lit it, he carried it around the room, reciting prayers, occasionally whipping the air with his prayer beads and cursing. Finally, the whole room was filled with fragrant smoke and the evil jinns were gone. Then he sat down and pulled out a bottle of saffron essence, a sheet of paper that had been soaked in ambergris, and a white pheasant feather quill. He dipped the quill in the saffron essence and wrote a prayer on the paper. He said Effat shouldn't leave the house for seven days and seven nights or else she would be possessed by jinns again. Everyone was happy. Her father kissed the prayer writer's hand and put some money, bread, and some chicken in a little bundle for him.

As the Soothsayer was gathering his things, Effat walked toward him and took his hand kindly. Then she smiled at the panic-stricken Soothsayer, and staring him in the eye, she exhaled deeply. Suddenly a wild fragrant perfume rose from her breath as though thousands of wild primroses and violets had sprouted from her mouth and filled the room that, until that moment, had just smelt of incense. It was a cool, intense smell. Terrified, the Soothsayer yanked his hand back. One of the villagers yelled, "That's the smell!! . . . The smell of black love. Run!" Everyone, the Soothsayer in the lead, was trying to escape when an old woman among them suddenly stopped. She leaned on her cane, closed her eyes, and inhaled deeply. Effat laughed. The old woman laughed too and motioned for her to come nearer. Effat approached timidly. Now the two of them were standing on the porch while the others were gathered around the frozen courtyard. One villager said to the old woman, "Come on! . . . Get away from her . . . You'll go crazy too." But ignoring the others, the old woman told Effat, "Exhale again. Do it for me." Effat took the old woman's hand gently in her own, inhaled deeply, and when she exhaled it felt as if spring was pouring from her mouth. The old woman closed her eyes and, in an instant, memories of her childhood and youth came from very far away and took their place in her mind and soul: running in the rice paddies, picking wild greengages, the flavor of raspberries bursting in her mouth, and the first time she made love. The old woman opened her eyes and laughed. Then she threw her cane aside and began spinning in a *chakkeh*; just like her fourteen-year-old self when the very same village leader was in love with her and had brought a bouquet of wild lilies to put in her hair.

It was Issa who first noticed the four o'clock plants that had begun to sprout and bloom. The greengage trees began to grow fresh leaves and blossom even though they were covered with snow, and suddenly the whole courtyard, covered in a blanket of winter snow just minutes before, was drowning in marigolds, primroses, and four o'clocks. Issa was so alarmed he began hiccupping, and if Homeyra Khatun hadn't brought him essence of orange blossom so that he could hold his breath for seven 'peace be upon hims,' who knows what disaster would have befallen him. After the shock of what was unfolding before his very eyes, and a hiccup that was so loud the chickens took flight, he laughed. Then his father, crying at the same time, laughed out of frustration and despair, and then one by one, villagers began to laugh until finally all of them, though still terrified, laughed. Laughed. Laughed.

People emerged from their houses and courtyards to watch, wide-eyed, as Sun Rose bushes, jasmine, and honeysuckle vines grew up the walls and trees in the dead of winter and, with the one little smile from Effat, burst into bloom. The perfume of spring flowers filled the air, the sound of laughter spread from Effat's house to the neighbor's house, and from the neighbor's house to the next house, and then through the length and breadth of the village. Everyone picked a flower and put it in their hair. Everyone began to sing and dance with a bloom in their hands. Everyone fell to their knees in the streets and showered God with words of adoration. Everyone knocked on a neighbor's door and placed a flower in the hand that emerged.

Effat stood on the porch observing everything closely. The

Soothsayer was dancing and laughing the most. Homeyra Khatun, her father, her brother, the neighbor girls, the village's moody young men, nagging old women, the weak, critical old men; all were dancing and laughing. Effat looked her fill then descended the porch steps and walked towards the path behind the house. From there she went towards the forest and walked and walked and walked until she reached the village's big tree. At least ten grown men needed to link arms to encircle that tree. It was getting dark. She sat down right there on the hill beside the tallest tree in the region and listened to the faint sounds wafting up from the people in the village, still laughing and dancing. She leaned against the tree and looked at the village below and thought, *Now, everyone knows what it means to be two.* Quietly humming local love songs, she calmly cleared away the snow and collected fallen twigs and branches. When she had made a huge pile, she set it alight and sat down for a while to let it catch. Grow. Intensify. And then, with utter tranquility and without even looking back at her village or house, she walked with steady steps into the fire. Smiling as though she had gone to stand beside a wood stove on a cold winter day, she let the fire penetrate to her bones. A place that would not leave any life. She smiled at her other; at her other who was playing the flute and watching his innocent lambs and sheep in the wide green Kalimani plains, and was thinking to himself how suddenly happiness can come and take you by surprise: the very moment that you realize that you are your innocent white lamb, and your innocent white lamb is you. You are that tree and that tree is you; that leaf; that fallen leaf you tread upon as you play the flute for your sheep and a walk in the plains.

Suddenly, the night sky over the village was filled with embers. Bright, shining embers that, like the tail of Halley's comet, flew slowly from the direction of the forest, from the direction of the big tree and fell on the villagers. As they were singing and laughing under the steady fall of embers, the villagers saw the Soothsayer collecting wood and piling it up in the village square. Then he lit a match and put it under the hollow, dry wood. The flames surged and grew. All the villagers sat around the fire and were silent for the first time since their wild laughter; as though their jaws hurt from all that laughing; as though all that joy had tired them out. The Soothsayer began reciting incantations. Ancient Pahlavi incantations. His arms outstretched under the shower of heavenly fire, he danced and sang around the flames, and let the embers rain down on his face and body and turn into light, brittle ash. Slowly, the villagers started dancing with him. They also sang incantations. Who would have thought that Pahlavi still existed in a part of each of their beings so many hundreds of years after their conversion to Islam. After that, it wasn't clear who went and brought wine or from where. Old, seven-year-wine. Everyone, from young to old, took a cup of wine as they sang incantations and danced, as though they were Zoroastrians from thousands of years before, who had never been converted to Islam, who were drinking wine in the square, dancing, and thanking nature and God with their joy. The old Soothsayer first poured a bit of the wine on the ground as had been tradition for thousands of years, drank the rest, and quoted a verse by Hafez:

Your beauty in pre-eternity appeared in a ray of God's light
Love was created and caught the whole world on fire.

Then without so much as looking back, without looking at the villagers or his ancestral home, he entered the fire and from its center stared at a point above him until he was consumed by flames.

The villagers didn't panic or cry; they weren't afraid. All were in a state of singular bliss as though suddenly they had achieved

Certainty. Certainty of the existence of the other. Certainty about the existence of the other in themselves. Certainty about that which they had thought was life but wasn't life at all. Then suddenly Issa's father took on the Soothsayer's role and continued chanting ancient incantations. Dancing, the people repeated the chants with him. Just then, the sound of cowbells could be heard approaching. Indian gypsies who came every year to pitch their tents for several days, sell their wares to the villagers, and tell their fortunes, emerged from the forest paths in an untimely fashion with their loads of cloth, nails, sickles, and copper dishes.

When the swarthy men and women descended from their cows, camels, horses, and mules, and saw the inhabitants of Razan standing around the fire, speaking in a tongue they hadn't spoken a year ago, and drinking wine, they stood open-mouthed staring at the people who, unlike every year, hadn't even noticed their cacophonous entry. At the same time, Issa's father recited:

> *Wisdom desired a light from that flame of love*
> *With a bolt of love's fervor the world was in tumult.*[30]

The villagers repeated the poem together with him and, upon the completion of the verse, they all stepped into the fire together, without looking back. Not one of them looked back. Not one of them thought of their children, or their spouses, or their parents . . . Not one of them glanced at their homes . . . They stepped into the fire as though to do anything else would have been senseless and meaningless. Having overcome their initial shock, the gypsies ululated. They yelled. They screeched, shook their bangles in the air, and hit them-

---

[30] A verse by Hafez.

selves over the head. They ran towards the fire and each one pulled someone away from the fire. Then they rushed to draw water from the well in the village square to quench the flames. In the blink of an eye they dispersed the villagers and pulled them into the dark alleyways. An hour later . . . nobody was left in the square. It felt as if the dream, or spell, or the magic, that had come over Razan, had passed and was gone. Issa, crouched in a corner, trembling, chilled to his core, and stared in silence at all that had happened right before his eyes and thought, *It's as though the Soothsayer never existed, Dad never existed, Effat never existed . . . there was no fire . . . and no love.*

From the next day, for forty days, no one in the village looked at anyone else. Nobody said hello or goodbye to anyone else. From the next day for forty days, snow, heavier than it had ever been before, bound everyone to their houses. Cows and sheep were imprisoned in their stables and died of starvation. It seemed as though spring never existed. Summer. Autumn. Nothing.

CHAPTER 12

Beeta, embittered, humiliated, and lost, stepped with sure and steady steps towards an unsure future as she thought about how the Revolution had changed her family's destiny, *her* destiny. She recalled a day at the height of the turmoil when she had seen through the high windows of her ballet class, people's feet rhythmically pounding the pavement outside, and shouting, "Death to the Shah! Death to the Shah! Deeeeeeeath tooooo the Shaaaaaaaah! Death to the Shah! Death to the Shah! Deeeeeeeath tooooo the Shaaaaaaaah!" A teacher from a neighboring classroom ran up to Beeta's teacher and whispered something in her ear. Then the other teacher yanked a headscarf from her purse, put it on, and left to join the protesters. Beeta's teacher, however, stayed put and repeated decisively, "Your jeté foot at forty-five degrees to the right foot and hands in fifth position! Exhale deeply and feel your breath as you guide it out from your heart." Just minutes later, some of the same people who had been marching came and dragged her teacher outside, and began beating and kicking her in the street. Screaming obscenities at the students, they drove them out of the classroom, and their ballet classes ended forever. She wondered what her teacher was doing now. Maybe she should try to find her when she got back to Tehran. Maybe she had left Iran or maybe all her talent for dance had gone to waste in the back rooms of her house as she cooked, sewed, and swept the floor.

Beeta looked around, trying to discern a path amid the trees and bushes. She saw nothing but green. Green leaves. Green branches. Green grass, and when, out of frustration, she turned to the sky to guess the way using the sun's path, she saw me coming slowly towards her. I showed her the way and tried to lift her spirits. But in the next moment, words spilled from my mouth that, instead of offering comfort, came out as a rebuke of her not thinking to say goodbye before she left. Her angry response that since I am everywhere, hellos and good-byes are meaningless, made me reach the bitter realization that, even if ghosts are loved ones, we are still nothing more than the forgotten dead. Determined not to let show, I asked instead what she would do, now. When she just shrugged her shoulders, I understood that her grievances against me, and life, ran much deeper.

What I said next caught even me off guard. "Life is usually determined in our absence which people find vexing. Don't you realize, though, how fortunate you are? At least you can still use your feet to walk, feel things with your skin, taste *ghormeh sabzi* and *abgoosht*. And you're stupid not to realize that even making love once is to taste a moment of bliss that can enrich your whole life!"

Before the last words had even completely left my mouth, she stopped and glared at me with such hatred that I was ashamed and horrified by what I had said, and made myself invisible. I couldn't believe I had uttered such a thing. Life had dealt us such harsh blows that we never had the opportunity to say hurtful things to one another. However, now that those words had actually come out, I couldn't bear hearing her contemptuous response: that she was outraged by my secretly watching all of her lovemaking over the last months, and she knew it. I was embarrassed that, since I was dead, I was capable of silently observing her private moments and those of others.

I let her continue on her own, but cried quietly to myself—

I did not want her to see my tears. I let her curse me from a distance, but she did not hear my own expletives. Hunched under a tree, my sobs resonating far into the distance, I realized that the quick succession of events in our family had left no time for me to cry. Beeta's look of hatred was a jolt that made me realize I was nothing but a delusional dead person; I could talk to the living and they could see me, but I was deceiving myself; my presence after death was a mere illusion. I thought that if I ever saw Sohrab again, I should tell him I'd made a mistake. I had been wrong to think that death only marked the end of some things. No! Death was the end of everything. The end of my body, my identity, my credibility. The end of everything that had meant something to me in life: family, love, trust, friendship. Yes . . . death was the end of all these things.

I cried until the stars came out and the jackals began to howl. I had cried so much, my head felt heavy. And then I felt the pressure of a hand on my shoulder. Death also had its advantages; nothing could frighten me: not even the pressure of an unknown hand on my shoulder, in the forest, in the dead of night. Impatiently, I lifted my head. It was the ghost of a middle-aged man. Unbidden, he sat down beside me and lay my head softly on his shoulder. I don't know why, but this made me cry even more. The man placed his hand on my head in a fatherly way, and I was happy he didn't ask anything. When my sobs had receded, indicating with his head, he said, "I was going to visit the river ghosts when I heard you. Join me if you'd like."

I went with him without thinking, and on the way, he explained that the river ghosts are people who had died in the nearby river and who came together, occasionally, to reminisce.

"What a useless thing to do!" I exclaimed impatiently. "Well, you have to pass the time somehow or else the loneliness becomes unbearable," the man replied. Wiping away the last of my tears, I said, "You sound just like the living." "Don't you see just how much we still live like the living?" he pointed out. "You're right. Perhaps we should change that. Either way, we're not alive enough," I replied despondently.

"Death hasn't made humans happier," the man said.

We continued in silence until we reached a river where a group of people was sitting around a fire. Among them was a ten-year-old boy who was wet and shivering, as though he had just come out of the river. One of the ghosts gave the boy his coat and murmured to the others, "He just drowned an hour ago. He doesn't know it yet."

I was looking at the boy's miserable, disbelieving eyes. The fire trembled in his pupils just as the novice ghost and little boy himself trembled in death's embrace. We were all in the arms of death and he alone didn't know it yet. He thought he was still in life's embrace. Still on the other side. The other side of the invisible wall. The little boy said he was a shepherd and that his name was Majid. He was crossing the river with his mother when he lost her. Again, everyone was silent. No one wanted to reminisce about life in the presence of Majid's novice ghost. They didn't want to rush his awareness of his own death. It had to happen naturally. I know, as I suppose everyone does, that the first hours of death are the worst; the hours you don't yet know you're dead, and if you do, you don't want to believe it. You can still sense your body's warmth, can feel the wetness of your tongue on your dry lips, and you know someone is nearby, waiting for you . . .

Then Majid asked, "What are you all doing here? Are you travelling?" We all exchanged looks, and hesitated, not knowing how to answer. At that very moment, several people approached, lantern in hand and alive. Majid's mother, father, and brother had come with a lantern to look for him on the banks of the river. Majid called out to them happily, flinging the coat off his shoulders and running towards them. We didn't move. He ran towards them but they were yelling out his name, and looking in a different direction; then they hurried away, as though they had found his body. Excited and over-joyed to be reunited, Majid caught up with them and threw his arms around his mother, but she kept crying and continued to walk away, not noticing Majid hanging onto her from behind. They came to a halt nearby and cried. Majid caught up with them again. Again, he tried. This time he embraced his father, but his father didn't pay any attention either. Walking right past him, his father hurled himself onto Majid's corpse and began sobbing. Majid finally caught sight of his own dead, wet, ice-cold face that had fallen limply onto his father's shoulder. Incredulously he looked at his own face. Then he took a step backwards. He looked at his hands and reached up to touch his face. Finally, he turned to stare at us. The middle-aged man who had spoken to me got up and, together with an old man, walked slowly towards the boy. But Majid seemed to have become aware that life and death were inseparable, that they were of one nature, and panicked. He ran away from them screaming, and disappeared into the forest.

For several minutes his terrified scream reverberated in my ears like a death knell. My chest tightened and right there in front of everyone, I wrapped my arms around my own loneli-ness and cried. A little later, the two men returned from the forest's dark interior with Majid's anxious ghost and sat him down next to me, once again wrapping their coats around him to take the edge off death's chill. He stared into the fire until he fell asleep in silence. I thought, poor Majid, poor me, poor all of us, the dead . . . because death has no release. When you're tired of life you can commit suicide to rid yourself of its trials, but what comes after death? It's not fair that in death, suicide isn't an option for liberation from its torments. The true definition of death is eternal boredom.

I looked at the sorrow and bewilderment of Majid's slack-muscled face. I wanted to take him into my arms like a sad little brother, comfort him and say, "Don't be sad. Tomorrow when you wake up, you'll see this is all just a dream. You'll milk the sheep alongside your brothers again and will guide them up into the high pastures with your father . . . Don't be sad, little brother. Soon you'll be so big that during one of the migrations you'll see a beautiful dark-eyed girl and you'll fall in love with her, not with one but with a hundred hearts. Then, while you're separated from her, you will fall ill, have a lump in your throat and a tightness in your chest and, not even the sound of your father's flute will bring joy to your heart. You'll want to listen to sad songs, and so you'll learn how to play the flute, and will play melancholy songs until the next migration. Then you will see that beautiful girl again. Now you will even know her name and, seeing the curves of her body moving away oblivious of you, you will know from now on that life without her would be meaningless. And so setting embarrassment aside, you tell your father everything, with anxious eyes. After that, everything is arranged much more quickly and simply than you imagined. You ask for her hand. She becomes your wife. You build a wooden house with your own two hands, and a year later you will have one child, three years later another, and four years later another still. Then one day, without knowing how it could possibly have arrived, a day will come when your son comes to you with anxious eyes, and says he has fallen in love with a dark-eyed girl during the migration. You go and propose marriage for your son, and with the birth of your fifth grandchild, on a day as ordinary as any other of life's exceedingly ordinary days, you die. That's it. Just like right now."

The river ghosts began recounting their memories and wanted me to tell my story, too. I explained everything briefly and then said I had to hurry back to my sister who was alone in the forest. At that moment, Majid, who had apparently heard my every word, opened his eyes and said, "I saw your sister looking for a long vine." Terrified, we rushed to her, and found her breathing ragged from the pressure of the thick vine around her neck, her fingers and toes twitching as her nerves fired. Just as death is a nightmare for the living, so too it is for the dead. I didn't want Beeta to join me on this side so soon, and I was determined not to let her. She still had many things to see to, although at this moment, she was too distraught to know this. As soon as she regained consciousness, she slapped me twice, which made me laugh. I had cried so much I couldn't contain my laughter. Then we wept in each other's arms until she fell asleep; we let the melancholy forest ghosts sit around us, patiently sympathetic.

When she awoke, we were all sitting around the fire keeping her warm under a pile of our coats. Majid was the first to speak to her and asked, "Do you really think life is that bad?" Beeta was staring at the fire and, by the way her lips were pressed together, it was clear she was still lost in thought. An old man asked a middle-aged man to tell of his life. "I've never told my story because I don't know how to," the middle-aged man said. "What do you mean?" the old man replied. "Everyone tells their story one way or another. Go on." To which the middle-aged man said, "Okay, I'll try. But I'm telling you right now, I don't know how to tell it like all of you."

His eyes riveted on the flames, in one single sentence, without pause, he began and ended as follows: We were three brothers who lived together in a house with our wives and children and aging mother and father and we made a living fishing and chopping wood until one day my little brother came home and said he had found a treasure map and asked us his two brothers to help him find the treasure but our old mother and father became sad and said they would disown us if we went treasure hunting because treasures are always jinxed and no one who goes looking for treasure ever comes back but we did not have ears for such talk and we didn't even listen to our father who told us that one day a boy bid farewell to his family to search for treasure but spent so much time going from village to village and from city to city that finally he became desperate and broke into the home of a rich man but was arrested and sent to jail and from there he sent a message to his father saying father come to my rescue for I am in prison but his father answered I told you not to go looking for treasure for you will only run into trouble and now there is nothing that I can do with one foot in the grave except tell you to come back when you have served your sentence for I have hidden a treasure in the grove for you which is the result of a lifetime of toil but do not take this for granted and do not squander it and upon hearing this the son could hardly contain his joy and then with his time in prison over he returned to the village and began digging in the grove for treasure but the more he dug the less he found until eventually he had dug up the whole grove without any sign of treasure but his mother had followed along behind him planting seeds in the tilled soil and very soon the garden became green and flourished and the plants grew and after a time they had a harvest and sold it and became quite wealthy and the son remembered his father's lesson to value the wealth and treasure of the earth and their health but our father's story fell on deaf ears and we bid them farewell and walked and walked and walked until we reached the place on the map that corresponded to this very river and we crossed it and continued until we reached a very tall tree on a hill with a fish carved into the north side of its trunk and if you stood in that direction you could see another very tall tree on a hill that we knew had the next symbol and so we continued until we reached the tree which had a turtle carved into it and we proceeded in the direction the turtle's head was pointing until we reached a large boulder from on top of which we could see a waterfall in the distance so instead of resting we continued to the waterfall and walked through the water entering a cave on the other side and in the heart of its dark interior gold and jewels shone bright as day so happy and cheering we filled our satchels and pockets and bags with jewels but we hadn't yet left the cave when two pigeons flew in and sat beside me on a rock and began speaking to each other and one said to the other those two poor brothers who don't know the other wants to kill them and the other pigeon said you are right sister those two poor brothers but really as you make your bed so you must lie in it and the other said you are right sister come let's leave these humans be and since I was sitting near them I heard and was surprised and told my two brothers that two pigeons had come and were sitting on a rock and saying that one of us will kill the other two and then I naïvely added I'm not planning to kill either of you because you are brothers of my own flesh and blood and anyway there is enough treasure here to make the people of a whole country happy so it's certainly enough for the three of us but my youngest brother said pigeons can't even talk so you probably invented the story to prepare us and you plan to kill us but when I tried to defend myself my second brother also attacked me saying apparently you really want to kill us right here but I brought a poisoned dagger to defend myself against the two of you and before he had finished speaking he was threatening the two of us with the knife but we yelled are you insane I was just telling you what I heard but let's just say you were right and I was lying and there were no pigeons because it was a test and you both failed but as soon as the words had left my mouth my youngest brother began laughing and joking and said he had just been joking too and just wanted to pull our legs and when our middle brother saw this he re-sheathed his dagger and he said it just reminded him of a story he heard years ago about three brothers who go to a mountain in search of a treasure which they find in the depths of a cave but the eldest brother throws his other two brothers

into a nearby well and takes the treasure unaware that it was
no ordinary well but was inhabited by jinns and fairies who
help the poor brothers take revenge on the eldest brother
when they hear what had happened and so one of the jinns
turns himself into a beautiful woman and waits where the eldest brother would pass and when the eldest brother sees her he
falls in love with not one but a hundred hearts and takes her
home and marries her but the woman says she will only marry
him on the condition that he never come to her room or have
anything to do with her between twelve at night and five in the
morning and if he fails he would be killed and the eldest
brother accepted the condition and so every night the woman
went into another room and from twelve at night until five in
the morning she kept the door shut until one night his curiosity got the better of him and he entered the room to find her
drinking wine and singing and dancing with a group of male
and female jinns so he fell into a jealous rage and as he was
about to kill the woman and the jinns with a sword the woman
turned back into her real self and put the sword to his throat
to kill him but the terrified man begged her don't kill me I will
be a dog at your door but don't kill me and when the woman
heard this she immediately turned him into a dog and from
that day since he has guarded the house of his two brothers as
a dog but when our middle brother told this story I became
angry and said tell the truth why did you mention this story
could it be you're really plotting something and we started
arguing when suddenly two big black dangerous snakes slithered out from under the gold and jewels and lunged at us and
when our little brother saw them he jumped up onto a big rock
and our middle brother killed one of them with his poison-
tipped dagger and I killed the other with a large stone as it was
trying to reach my little brother to bite him and so I saved him
and all three of us were happy because it had made us closer
and we forgot all that had been said before and we hurried

excitedly back until we reached this very river where we splashed water onto our faces and our little brother filled his flask and we set off again and walked and walked and walked until we were close to home when our little brother said come let's rest a bit and he pulled the flask from his satchel and gave it to us to drink and we drank and that very moment our middle brother starting foaming at the mouth and died instantly and I passed out and with half-open eyes I saw my little brother gather our bags of jewels give us a kick and head towards home but it was God's will that I lived and that my father found me half-dead the next day and carried me home and nursed me back to life and although I was so weak I couldn't even get out of bed I could hear what was being said namely that my little brother had told Mother and Father that three black snakes had attacked us near the house and that our middle brother and I had died from snake bites but that he was able to escape the third snake and make it home but later I heard Father say that something seemed fishy when our little brother had fearfully taken his wife and children and left the house forever and Father then came searching for our bodies and he eventually found me barely alive next to my brother's body and took us home and then I heard him say to my mother what a story the little brother invented and in all these years we have never seen a poisonous snake here so how could he say three poisonous snakes attacked them and once my father left the room my mother went to my wife and said something isn't right and her gut is telling her that our little brother killed our middle brother and poisoned me but when our middle brother's wife heard this from my wife she began hitting herself and crying and said she had disliked our little brother from the very beginning because he was sneaky and sly and from that night forth she went to bed sighing and asking God to finally give him what he deserves but my poor parents were left with a corpse on their hands and so began to dig a grave behind the house and buried my brother there and planted forget-me-nots but by the time they had woken up in the morning all the flowers had been burned from the roots and were black so my old mother and my second brother's wife got to work and this time they brought primroses from the forest and planted them over his grave but the next day they saw that their roots too were burnt and their flowers black and so on the third day they went to meadow and forest and brought back wild violets and planted them and the next day they found that these flowers had grown and sprouted new shoots and so immediately my mother and my brother's wife knew that my middle brother wanted revenge because we believe wild violets mean revenge and so we also understood that my brother's ghost was extremely angry and would not rest easy until he had taken his revenge and when my parents finally completed the burial and finished mourning they turned all their attention to me and prayed every day and cursed and disowned my little brother but I was getting thinner and older by the day until all my hair had turned grey and my wife had completely given up hope that I would get well again but my parents had not given up hope and were constantly invoking the Gazou Brothers and their shrine to cure me and one day when I was nothing but skin and bones they carried me with their old infirm bodies on a small bed to the sacred shrine of the Gazou Brothers in a distant place on a mountain so that I might be cured there on high and I was so sick and weak my only desire was to regain my health to return my parents' kindness and make up for their suffering and so I prayed and with tears flowing I implored God and the Gazou Brothers to cure me so I might be a cane on which my parents could lean but at the same time my father prayed for me and said we do not want you to be cured for us we want you to be cured so that you can be alongside your wife and children but my mother scolded both of us saying I don't want you to be cured for us or your wife but for yourself but what would you know Huma—the bird of happiness that grants your wish if it flies over you and hears it—flew over me at the exact moment I said I wanted to stay alive and be healthy to be a cane on which my mother and father could lean and therefore just then and while my parents were arguing I fell asleep and they left me alone in one of the sacred rooms of the shrine to sink into a sacred slumber in which I could see my fate and so it happened that I instantly fell into a deep sleep and dreamed that I was lying on the road somewhere between the two tombs of the Gazou Brothers shrine dreaming that I was sitting on the road between the tombs of the Gazou Brothers shrine lost and crying and unsure of which brother to ask for a cure when a radiant figure with a green turban appeared above me and taking my hand lifted me from the ground and said why are you crying and I said I am sick and want healing but he said there is nothing wrong with you and he put some candies in my mouth and at the same time another shining man with a white turban approached from the other direction put a hand on my head and poured some cool water into my mouth to drink and placed five candies in my right hand and said starting tomorrow eat one of these every day and serve your parents in your health then both of the shining men departed in opposite directions and I awoke and found myself lying on the road in between the two tombs of the Gazou Brothers and I looked around confused when suddenly I woke up again to find myself in one of the rooms of the shrine of the Gazou Brothers and I stood up with a strength I hadn't had for months and I found a mirror and saw that my hair was again completely black and as I was about to run my fingers through it joyfully I saw five candies fall from my right hand to the floor and when I saw them I began to scream and cry and unable to believe what had happened I fainted and when I regained con-sciousness I saw my parents sitting beside me crying having realized upon seeing my black hair that I had seen a holy figure and had been cured and when I told them about the five candies they cried even harder and we all washed and stood to face Mecca and cried and said a prayer of thanks and suddenly I felt so hungry that I ate all the food they could bring and still asked for more and so my mother and father happily went to ask others who had come to pray at the shrine for food and told them what had happened and groups of people brought me food and tied pieces of cloth on my arms legs and in my hair and ripped off shreds of my clothes for their own healing and intercessions and I didn't even notice them because I hadn't eaten anything for months and now that I had been cured by the power of the shrine for the two Gazou brothers the food tasted and smelt so good I couldn't think of anything else especially since some of them had prepared *gheimeh* as an offering and I like someone who had never eaten it before, inhaled the scent of the cinnamon and saffron and split peas and lamb to remember the flavor of life and I will never forget the pleasure with which I poured some sauce over a piece of *tahdig* with turmeric and with closed eyes placed it in my mouth and the crunch echoed in the room and I was truly savouring it and when I opened my eyes and saw all those people kneeling on the floor looking at me with amazement I started laughing and everyone looked at one another unsure of what to do but I continued laughing until the sound of my laughter carried over the hills and forests and reached the village and house where my little brother was living and he heard it and out of fear said the Shahada because he realized that I was alive and had returned from the dead but my laughter again carried through the hills and forests and came up to the Gazou shrine and entered the room and reached me and when I heard my own laughter I began suddenly to weep and sob loudly and all the people were reminded of their own misery and began crying and our tears were so abundant they covered the floor and formed a stream that flowed out of the room on to the terrace to the base of a barren mulberry tree that was said to have been planted hundreds of years ago by the Gazou brothers themselves and suddenly in the middle of summer this barren tree began to blossom and an hour later the blossoms fell off and were replaced by large white mulberries that were sweeter than any mulberries we had ever eaten and so from then on the people named it the sorrow-opening tree and every year people tie cloth to its branches and ask for their prayers to be answered and well that's how I was cured and I left the mountain with my parents to go home but what would you know word had spread from shepherds to fishermen from fishermen to woodchoppers from woodchoppers to villagers near and far that I had been cured in the shrine of the Gazou Brothers and so all along the way groups of people were waiting for me to pass to go instantly mad and scream and yell at the sight of me and attack me to rip off a piece of my clothing for their oblations and for the healing of their sick children and relatives and then when my clothing was nothing more than shreds in their hands they shed tears and said peace be upon you and left to spread the news until it reached my brother and when my brother heard I had been cured with his own ears and was completely certain that I was alive he told his wife he had to apologize to me or else I might want to kill him but his wife said it was no use and even if he asked for forgiveness I would still kill him and so they saw no other option but to run away and so from then until the time I was murdered they moved like vagabonds from city to city from village to village because they were constantly afraid I would come after them to kill them whereas God had given me a new lease of life and I didn't even think about them my only desire was to serve my mother and father who had never given up hope for me and I didn't even pay much attention to my wife and children who were very kind to me until one of God's many ordinary days when I no longer thought of my brother or death my father died and several days later my mother too and I was still mourning the death of my dear parents when I came to this river to fish and forget a bit of the sorrow unaware that my brother had not stopped thinking of me and had been hiding near the house he attacked me from behind with an axe killing me and throwing my body into this very river in this very spot and he buried the axe in this corner here and so it was that I finally died and my life came to an end but the ghost of my second brother who finally had an opportunity to take revenge set to work and every night he digs up the axe and places it under my little brother's pillow and he finds it every morning and terrified and half-dead spends half the day returning to this place to re-bury the axe and then go back to the village in the hope that it will stay put but the next morning he again finds it under his pillow and this is the only thing my brother's ghost does every night taking immense pleasure in our youngest brother's suffering.

The man finally finished his long sentence, took a deep breath, and stared into the fire. Nobody said a word; all looked into the fire in silence. Finally, I said, "What a story!"

Another man said, "My concentration didn't falter for even a second." The middle-aged man blushed in embarrassment and asked, "I'm sorry, is this how people tell stories?" The old man answered, "Yes, this is one way people do it."

I looked at the eyes of the ghosts sitting around the fire and at Beeta, and suddenly I realized that we dead are the sorrowful side of life, while the living are the joyful side of death. And yet, Beeta was not joyful and it was the sad side of life that she didn't even know she should be joyful in life because there was nothing else she could do. I wanted to tell her this, but was afraid of bringing her damaged spirit down even further. Fortunately, she herself eventually spoke and said, "It seems that from among you, I am the more fortunate because nobody killed me. But I don't feel happy at all." She looked at we who had died. The dead who had been the first to meet her in the world of the living outside Razan. An old man in the group responded, "This is because you don't yet realize how beautiful, young, and healthy you are." Beeta smiled and her cheeks reddened by the light of the fire in silent emotion; and all of us who were dead saw how good the smile looked on her. But as she recalled dark memories, her smile faded and she said, "But the man who loved me simply turned his back on me and married a young girl." The middle-aged man said, "All the better! It means you were lovable enough but he wasn't smart enough to realize it."

Beeta wore the smile of a bewildered woman who didn't know whether to be happy or sad. In the end, she said, "What do you say I should do? My mother, with whom I am extremely upset right now, left—" Pointing at me she continued, "My little sister and big brother were killed, and I left my lonely old father to go to Tehran; but I don't even know what I'm going to do once I'm there." "Go, be strong," the old man said. "And any time you despair, think of us; we are eternal but joyless, while you are mortal but joyful."

Beeta was clearly heartened a bit by these words and I thought what lonely people we had been, living for years without anyone around to see us beyond the family tragedies, to praise us, and give us the strength to continue living. And it was thus that after a long pause, Beeta suddenly turned to me, sitting opposite her on the other side of the fire, and with a courage I didn't know she had, said, "Forgive me for not being the sister I should have been. You were a sister to me in ways that even went beyond what you were capable of. Because of us, you even continue to live alongside us and protect us. During the years of the black snow, who would have brought us wood and food, if you hadn't? If you hadn't gone to see Sohrab in prison, who else would have been able to go and comfort him? And most importantly, if you hadn't come back to us after your death, how would we have been able to bear the sorrow of losing you?" Then she paused and, embarrassed, continued, "But from now on, how about with me you respect the boundaries of life and death."

The Holy Gospel begins thus: *In the beginning was the Word.* And the word is so heavy that it can bear the weight of creation and all existence on its shoulders. Just like right now when the weight of Beeta's words were making me aware of the limits of my breadth. "What you ghosts said tonight showed me that I am not strong enough," she continued. "You have to be extremely strong to live among the living." Then turning to me again, she said, "That's why I don't want you to come checking on me until the day I go back to Razan. Let me come to understand what it means for a living person to be alone in the true sense of the word; let me find my own way. If I survive the throngs of people in Tehran, you will see me again in Razan, and if I die, I'll also come looking for you to say just how precious your existence beyond life and death has been."

And so it was that kissing Beeta on the cheek as we said goodbye, I was anxious it would be our last meeting, unaware that she would be the only one of we three siblings to survive, albeit in the depths of the Caspian Sea.

CHAPTER 13

fterwards, I took the road towards Dad and solitude,
while Beeta took the road to the city and its hustle and
bustle. She left with the innocent face of an anguished
girl, and returned with the expression of a stalwart woman;
with several grey hairs, a few wrinkles in the corners of her
eyes, lips that were accustomed to silence, and feet that had
covered long distances. Moreover, her account of the events of
the last several years was so succinct we didn't dare ask more.
She seemed to have become inexplicably accustomed to keeping silent. I didn't blame her. When she described how she had
joined the first student dissent group upon enrolling at the university as a student of art history, and was arrested at a student
protest, banned from studying, and then sent to prison, we
realized that life still had yet grimmer things in store for the
members of our family. It had taken her less than an hour to
recount everything from start to finish; and then, at the end, as
she went to the kitchen to pour herself and us some tea, she
wrapped it all up with two bits of news: Uncle Khosrow, whom
I'd been expecting to see in Razan for years, and had been
arrested because of his mystical beliefs, was finally out of
prison but had immediately and indefinitely left Iran for India,
without being able first to say goodbye. He left to live out the
rest of his life in one of India's thousands of strange and fan-
tastic temples, and seek the nature of God in the unity of its
seventy-seven religions. Second, that the mayor of Tehran, still
trying to get his clutches on the city's old estates, was resorting

to threats and bribes, but Granddad and Great Granddad were determined to die in the house where they were born.

The whole time Beeta was giving us headline-like snippets of prison and arrest, Uncle Khosrow's self-imposed exile, and the city's threats, my gaze was unwavering, locked on Beeta's pained eyes, prematurely aged with experience but innocent with youthful disbelief, as she attempted to show how ordinary all the bad news was. Had she wanted, perhaps she could have recounted everything in detail, like the middle-aged ghost, without interruption or pause, but she had decided otherwise. Brevity is a response to suffering, and she wanted to be strong. Perhaps that was the reason she had become so prone to silence. She didn't want to prolong the suffering that affected us any longer. She wanted to be in the present as much as possible. Yes, Beeta had changed. She had lived through suicide and gone on to interact with the living. And so it was, that after several weeks of relaxation and wandering in the garden around the circles of scorched earth, reliving memories she didn't want to share, she began leafing through Dad's old magazines. Books had always been the first and final refuge in our house. Contrary to my expectations, she didn't turn to books on politics or sociology, but directly to serialized stories of romance in popular magazines. It was then I realized that a person's seemingly unemotional exterior was no indication of their interior. Then, to my utter surprise, she began reading children's books. She gradually developed a great fondness for fairytales. She read all of Hans Christian Andersen, the Brothers Grimm, Mehdi Sabahi, Sadegh Hedayat, and Samad Behrangi, then turning to *One Thousand and One Nights*, the *Shahnameh*, *Darab Nama*, *Samak-e Ayyar*, *Amir Arsalan*, and *Hossein Kord Shabestari*. Reading all these long books took months. Then she began collecting photographs and paintings of sky fairies, mermaids, earth fairies, angels, jinns, and mythical demons. Finally, one day she found a five-hundred-page notebook and began writing an encyclopaedia—*Encyclopaedia of the Imaginary Creatures of Iran*—with no clue, herself, of where the idea had come from. The encyclopaedia grew bigger and bigger as time went on. The Al, Anqa,[31] Ashu Zusht, Bakhtak, Chamrosh[32] and Davalpa, to the Huma, Fairy King, First Cow, Mardazma,[33] Rokh, Shirdal, and Simourgh,[34] these and many others were featured. In comprehensive chapters devoted to the demons of Ancient Iran, she described Aktash, the demon of denial, who seems to destroy the earth and life, Apush the demon of drought, and Bushasp, the demon of deep sleep. The more she read old books such as *The Darab Nama*, *One Thousand and One Nights*, Khayyam's *Nowruz Nama*, *Hossein Kord Shabestari*, *The Shahnama*, *Eskandar Nama*, *Malek Jamshid*, *Jame al-Olum*, *Ajayeb Nama,* and *Aja'ib*

[31] *Al*, in folk belief, a creature that seeks to hurt women who have just given birth if they are left alone; *Anqa*, a mythical bird that lives on Qaaf mountain. When this bird desires a mate it lays an egg and flaps its wings over the egg with such vigor that, in the heat it has generated and its excitement of reaching its mate, the bird catches fire, burns, and turns to ash. The egg is fertilized by the ash and its offspring born. There can only ever be one Anqa at a time.

[32] *Ashu Zusht*, the name of a mythical Iranian owl. Ashu Zusht was created by the gods to oppose Ahriman. When he recites from the holy book the demons are frightened; *Bakhtak*, a night hag that, according to popular Iranian belief, tries to suffocate people in their sleep; *Chamrosh*, a giant bird in Iranian mythology that destroys Iran's enemies.

[33] *First Cow*, according to Iranian myth, is holy and pre-eternal. It was killed by Mithra so as to make the earth fertile through the flow of its blood; *Mardazma*, an Iranian mythical creature that sat on the side of the road and sought to test the bravery of passersby by frightening them. If a man was successful, the *mardazma* would become his friend; if the man failed he would be killed.

[34] *Rokh*, a mythical bird that lives atop Qaaf mountain and communicates with wind and light; *Shirdal*, a mythical Iranian creature with the head of a lion, body of a bird, and ears of a horse. Its duty was to guard the treasure of the gods; *Simourgh*, a giant bird that has its nest on the Tree of Life, which contains the seeds of all the earth's plants. The Simourgh knows the secret of existence.

va Ghara'ib, the deeper she delved into the magnificent expanse of ocean that was the Iranian people's real-imaginary beliefs, and became ever more detached from the real, day-to-day world. To deny or forget her past, she read and wrote, submerging herself in the meaning of myth, until one night as she was bathing, her eyes fell on her naked body. She spent long minutes looking at her reflection in the mirror and suddenly realized the futility of what she had begun. Her body, long in denial, had become accustomed to love and life, and with the recognition of that reality had begun to wilt. Try as she might, she couldn't recall when several large wrinkles had appeared under her eyes, one hundred and thirty-eight grey hairs had sprouted at her temples, or the skin on her upper arms had loosened. Try as she might she couldn't recall when one of her molars had rotted or her periods had been delayed. Emerging from the bathroom she went straight to the porch knowing she would find Dad there. She took his hand affectionately in her own, held it to her cheek, and said, "I think it'll be my turn soon." Sitting there looking at the circles still scorched in the grass, he looked at her listlessly and then, after a while, contrary to Beeta's expectation, a pale smile formed on his lips.

So, Beeta stopped reading and writing, and began to wait in anticipation. She didn't know what she was waiting for but she had no doubt the time would soon come and she would be ushered into a new, maddening chapter of her life. A point of no return. She thought of Charles Bukowski's words, *Find what you love and let it kill you.* To begin with, she stopped reading and writing. Perhaps it could be said that she stopped resisting, and eventually she stopped her silence. Years in Tehran had made her tough enough. Maybe enough was enough. So, she stopped monitoring herself, her thoughts, the grove, Dad, and finally gave in to that in which she had recently been drowning: fantasy.

She lay on the bed and fantasized about this new phase of

life. Ashamed, she thought maybe after all these years Issa would suddenly appear and they would go together to some distant place, forever. But immediately, she berated herself for being so foolish, for still thinking about him after all this time. Then she entertained herself with newer fantasies. She thought that maybe she would set off to search for Mom. She imagined herself going from city to city, showing people a picture of her, until one day a child would point out a house and she would see Mom with a new husband and kids, and she wouldn't recognize Beeta at all. Sometimes in her imagination, Beeta would miss who she no longer was and cry, and would curse Mom in her heart for leaving them like that, without any warning.

Once, after we had been sitting together at the edge of the forest for a long time, and had rolled cigarettes from the grass the way she had learned from Issa, and smoked and smoked, she said to me, "It's life's failure and its deficiencies that make someone a daydreamer. I don't understand why prophets and philosophers didn't see the significance in that. I think imagination is at the heart of reality, or at least, is the immediate meaning and interpretation of life." I was staring at her, thinking about her words. I was coming to the conclusion that she was changing, shedding her skin once again when she said, "Aren't dreams part of life's reality? Or desires? Who doesn't believe that the Huma bird, who made whoever it was flying over happy, really existed at one time? Or the Simorgh, to which the lives of Sam, Zal, and Rostam were bound. All these books have been written about it and all of these paintings painted. What's common to all of them?" She paused, gave a deep sigh, and then said finally, "I mean, when life is so deficient and mundane, why shouldn't imagination supplement reality to liven it up?"

Gradually her dreams became longer and her reveries increased. In the house's estrangement, she discovered a new world in her extreme efforts to prevent her dreams from evaporating. She spent hours tossing and turning in bed after waking up, or would sit and think about her dreams, connect them, and seek to understand them in books by Ibn Sirin, Jung, and Freud, or the fiction of Mircea Eliade, Mehrdad Bahar, or works by Lévi-Strauss, hoping for a clear idea of the path her future would take.

One night she dreamed she had turned into a fish and when she awoke the next day she said, "My dream was so realistic that I don't know if I'm a human who dreamed she was fish, or a fish who's dreaming she's a human." Although she expected to see signs of reality in her dreams, before the birth of the first fish, she had misinterpreted her dreams about the sea and fish.

Issa had once told her, "One day I will see you again when the dragonflies are mating." But when she asked when their mating season was he never answered. Yet Issa did keep his promise, and now on one of many spring nights, among dragonflies pregnant with sleep, they saw each other again for the last time, although, contrary to Beeta's expectations, this meeting didn't take place in a concealed corner of the grove encircled by flames. As it happened, when Beeta woke up in the morning she was sure she had spent all night making love to Issa. However, the more exact the details of his presence became, the less she could recall if Issa had come into her dream, or if she had entered his. But either way the result was the same. Soon she felt all the signs of pregnancy. The first child was born in the tumult of evaporating dreams, astonishment, and the anticipation of entering a new life phase, the nature of which was a mystery. What she least expected on the threshold of this new stage of life was born in the hush of the dead of night in her bedroom, and fitted in a small glass bowl. It was a little goldfish. Horrified, she placed the bowl on the shelf and decided not to say anything about it to Dad. Her second child was born in the morning. She was screaming in panic, "Why is my bed wet, and full of sand and scallops?!" The fish was still alive, and Dad, who was drawn into the room with all the commotion, very quickly pulled it out from the bloodied sheets and put it in the bowl on the shelf with the other. Soon we had to add fish tanks because every morning she gave birth to another goldfish. The house was full of tanks and bowls, both large and small, which were placed on shelves, in the corners, on Sohrab's empty bed and on mine, and even in Dad's workroom. It added to the weight of the house's isolation and estrangement. Like a large, lazy iguana, Dad had no choice but to crawl out from the leaden shadows and his sphere of oblivion several times a day to feed the poor animals. He thought to himself, "I could think of these as my grandchildren. My forlorn, scaled grandchildren."

Had she not come to her own rescue in time, Beeta might have bled to death one morning when a very large shell containing a giant pearl got stuck in her cervix. Once again, she was close to drowning in the sea within her body. It was thus that several months later, when she was awoken by the *slosh slosh* of water beneath her, she was not too surprised, but when she fell to the ground as she got out of bed, she was worried. Pulling herself across the floor, she made it to the wall and managed to reach the light switch. When the light came on she saw Zakariya Razi, our great ancestor, standing ankle-deep in water, leaning against the wall, and saying gleefully, "I found the solution. This way you're safe from 'them,' and so too, the trunk." Then before Beeta had the chance to say anything, he disappeared, happy and smiling, through the damp wall. Beeta's legs had been transformed into a fish tail.

It was marvelous and beautiful, but in the beginning the tail horrified her. She sat in a corner all day looking at it, and gradually discovered what the beautiful thing was capable of, but was left wondering how she was supposed to get to the kitchen to cook, or to the grove to direct the workers. I had to come out of my treehouse more than usual to check on her, and to reassure her that change was necessary to reach her dreams. At the beginning, Dad thought it would be best for Beeta to stay put and for things to continue as they were. That very same day he filled the large bathtub with water so Beeta could spend time there. Several days late, however, he saw the cruelty in this. Sitting in a bathtub for hours staring at white tiles wouldn't be anyone's idea of fun, so he hung some pictures on the bathroom walls and placed some flower pots in the corners. But he soon saw this, too, was useless. So, he decided to seal the bathroom door with cement and remove its roof and fill the whole bathroom with water so she could enter through the ceiling any time she wanted a swim. Then he released all the fish from the bowls into it, too; this way, at least, she could keep herself occupied with her children.

It was not easy. Any time Beeta needed to immerse herself into the bathroom 'pool,' Dad would hoist her up in a large tub over the walls, through the non-existent roof, with a rope and pulley he had installed that was as far as possible from the prying eyes of the villagers and people working in the grove. Beeta was delighted that she had inadvertently forced Dad to move about, although she was afraid these efforts would be temporary, and Dad would return to a state of inert silence. However, contrary to what she could have imagined, Dad then gave her all the shells he had collected during Sohrab's absence so she would have something in addition to the fish to keep her entertained; and he collected waterlilies from the swamp to grow in the water. Every day he brought her food through the roof. Finally, one day Dad called me over to help him build some steps and a balcony extending over the pool where the bathroom ceiling had been. It was thus that mealtimes gradually became enjoyable for all three of us. Dad would make food and, just like in the olden days when all five of us would picnic at the foot of Mt. Damavand, Darband, or the road to

Chalus, we spread our things out on the new balcony next to Beeta and, looking at the view as we ate, we would talk about our day; and in the absence of Mom and Sohrab, we sometimes allowed ourselves to laugh and watch how the fish were growing, and the grass, which was gradually filling in the scorched circles. But Beeta was changing. She wanted to stay in the bath twenty-four hours a day; and could no longer lie on her bed; instead she slept deep underwater in the bathtub. Then her skin began to change: gradually her arms and shoulders and face became covered with beautiful, tiny golden-silvery scales; and when we weren't looking, she would press herself against the walls of the bath to feed on tiny algae. Every afternoon, as we sat talking for hours, she said it had been easy for her to leave Dad in order to seek her own destiny, but now she was willing to endure her tight space so as not to leave him alone, again, to his immobility and silence.

It was thus that, during the day she would lie in the water in the sun, and at night she would sleep bathed in starlight, dreaming of the sea. She would play with the fish and shells, and lose herself for hours in the beauty of the waterlilies, while she would spend the rest of the day in lethargy and languor. She allowed herself to feel the long pauses between minutes, and quietly follow every minute movement of the clouds from the beginning of the break of dawn to the end of dusk. Once she told me of the extraordinarily poetic bliss of feeling blue sky drops on her skin and seeing with her own eyes how a prism of light on the lining of a cloud had turned a crow into a rainbow. Another time, lost in a white cloud in the middle of the blue sky, she said the best thing about Razan's sky is that the clouds' virginity hadn't yet been raped by airplanes.

In our mania for reading we could still get excited by and devour a newly discovered book. To keep Beeta entertained, we searched the house's nooks and crannies for forgotten works. Keeping them as dry as possible, she read them eagerly.

After a while she asked me to read them to her. It was clear that the shapes of letters and words were slowly losing meaning for her, but she was happy that she could still hear and understand and could still speak, as before.

During those days, we discovered and read *Nausea* and *The Metamorphosis* together—books that were followed by days of discussion. Beeta laughed, and was relieved that she hadn't turned into a disgusting giant beetle, like poor Gregor Samsa. These two books brought us closer together, again. Perhaps now that Beeta was transforming into an aquatic creature so as to experience and live life with a freedom that had been impossible as a human, she was better able to understand my experience as a ghost. Perhaps she could better understand that despite the laws of matter, ghosts still existed and our existence continued with equal intensity.

Nausea showed us what complex political, religious, and philosophical intermediaries the world has—a world we wanted to comprehend directly; *The Metamorphosis* showed two bereft girls that humankind today is not what classic literature had taught us.

We read *The Unbearable Lightness of Being* with such rapture that before we had realized what had happened, night had fallen, and *Scenes from a Marriage* made us cry over our naive belief in the purity of lovemaking. Eventually, Dad joined us, too, and together we explored *Lovers*, *Moderato Cantabile*, *The House of Sleeping Beauties*, *Ragtime*, *The Tatar Steppe*, *The Catcher in the Rye*, and *The Remains of the Day*, then discussed them for days. One day, with no other books left, we began Hervé Bazin's *Viper in the Fist* that had been found—forgotten—behind a bookcase. Never could we have imagined the masterpiece that lay in store. Things weren't always so idyllic, though. One stormy day, as Dad tried to climb up to the top of the bathroom wall, he slipped on the steps in the wind and rain and fell to the floor, spilling all the food. Beeta heaved herself up to lean over the edge of the wall to help, but she too slipped and landed next to Dad on the floor, tearing her delicate scales.

With sheets of rain pouring down onto their bleeding bodies, and blood mixed with the laboriously prepared eggplant stew seeping through the mud into the ground, Beeta sobbed and took Dad into her arms, begging his forgiveness for having been so selfish that she hadn't been prepared to suppress her dreams. But that very day Dad made up his mind. Despite what remained of our happiness, he could no longer bear seeing Beeta's life wasting away. Several days later, he suggested that it would be best for her to begin making preparations to go and live in the sea. Beeta insisted the song of the sea could nourish her from a distance and there was no need to actually go and live in it. But we all knew she was just saying that for our sakes.

Beeta's new stage of life had come upon her faster and more unexpectedly than she had imagined; and though she was resigned and receptive to all the changes, never for a moment did the sense of guilt leave her.

She constantly fretted about what Dad would do without her. She thought perhaps it would have been better to have refrained from giving in to her fantasies and dreams, to never have left Razan for Tehran, or to never have come back. That way at least she would have remained human and Dad would always have been able to hope she would one day return. But now she was never going to come back. She wondered if it would be better to ask our ancestor to turn her back into her original form, and so for three days she called to him in her heart, but he didn't appear. It was thus that, when the night had finally arrived, having dressed her in a *manto* and headscarf, hidden her tail under a blanket, and placed a bucket of water at her side so she could take a fresh breath if she needed, we reached a cozy spot on a dark beach, and bid her farewell.

All three of us were silent and anxious. Dad kissed her

slimy cheek and said comfortingly, "Have you noticed how beautiful freedom has made you? I like this beauty of yours." Then he took a rose-shaped necklace from his pocket that had belonged to Mom and fastened it around Beeta's neck, and said, "We wanted to give this to you for your wedding." Sitting on the damp sand and playing with the water, Beeta hesitated a bit. The sea was silver under the moonlight and stars. After a little while, she said quietly, "If you find Sohrab's grave one day, kiss it for me." Then all three of us cried and held one another in a tight embrace, smothering each another in kisses. I removed her headscarf and *manto* and threw them aside. Beeta entered the sea until she was half-submerged. Once she was neck-deep in water she removed her tank top and threw it to me, laughing. She had no idea what a splendid sight she was, from the shore. The moon and stars reflecting in the water around her, with her long wavy hair covering her breasts, and her beautiful tail making gentle ripples around her. In her excitement to plunge into the sea, the Caspian Sea, and to do so with such utter freedom, she did a somersault underwater and re-emerged bursting with laughter. Her beautiful laughter made us laugh too. She waved goodbye, but then couldn't bear it, and came back to the shore, and hugged us tightly. She whispered in my ear, "If Issa ever comes looking for me, tell him I'm back in Tehran." We looked at each other with tear-filled eyes and I thought, despite all the modern romances we had read, she was still in love with Issa, a classic kind of love.

Beeta swam further out, again. The sound of the waves filled the silence between us. Dad wanted to turn away and leave, but he couldn't. He ran into the water and held her tightly to his chest, sobbing onto her scale-covered shoulder. Beeta was his last living child . . . the person who still connected him to life. He inhaled the scent of her hair and kissed it, and this time without looking at her, he turned away; at the same time, enveloped by dark Caspian waves, without a thought to what had become of the trunk our ancestor had wanted her to protect, she swam away a distance, dipping her head in the water so that her salty tears mixed with the sea.

After that, Dad went to meet her on the shore every week with me occasionally in tow, and one day when Beeta asked me about Issa, I lied and said he'd come looking for her once. A tear rolled down her cheek. I didn't know if it was a tear of joy or anguish. On later visits, other merpeople came as well; lantern in hand, their women with beautiful breasts, and long, seductive hair, and their men with stalwart features and kind expressions. Dad was happy to see Beeta had made friends and had been accepted in her new environment. The Caspian merpeople sometimes came up onto the shore to sit beside us and talk. Under our careful and curious observations, we saw Beeta gradually changing. She not only stopped asking about Issa, but she even mentioned Mom and Sohrab less. Every time we met her, she seemed more joyful and carefree, even playful, than she had been the time before. We attributed this to the pleasure of freedom in her new environment; the pleasure of finally being able to do what she wanted—to swim freely. But the day one of the mermaids spoke with Dad, we realized the differences between their world and ours weren't just on the surface.

The mermaid asked Dad, who hadn't shaved for a while and whose beard was now as grey as his hair, "Why are you always sad?" When Dad didn't answer, she continued, "In our world, nobody comes into life to stay forever, and our fish-like minds don't allow us to think of the past. If you live in this way, you'll never become sad." Once she had said this, she threw herself playfully into the water and disappeared into the sea, along with Beeta and the rest of the merpeople. And so the more dependent Dad became on seeing Beeta and enjoying her sense of freedom and merrymaking, the fewer the visits became. Not because Beeta was busy with other things, but because she had developed a fish-like forgetfulness.

The day came when Beeta approached the shore but didn't get out of the water. Instead, she watched us suspiciously from behind a large rock. She dived underwater and then re-emerged, again hiding behind the rock and sneaking peeks at us. Finally, I jumped into the water. When I reached her I said, "What's wrong with you?"

Anxiously she asked, "Who are you?" When I introduced myself and told her the necklace she was wearing had been Mom's, she thought a bit, and finally breaking into a smile, said, "I knew I had to come here for something but no matter how hard I thought about it I couldn't tell who you were."

The next time Dad and I went to the beach, Beeta didn't show up although we sat waiting until dawn before returning home, in silence. Realizing that Beeta was living pure, mermaid-like moments in the present—what mystics dream of—Dad never again set foot on that deserted Caspian beach.

That next day, Dad walked through the house, completely broken-hearted, then climbed up to the balcony to peer down on the small fish in the bathroom. As the following morning dawned, he went out under the tiny drops of rain, and began digging. I was watching him from my treehouse. At first I thought he'd been gripped by a new mania and wanted to bury himself alive, but when I saw that the pit he was digging grew bigger and bigger, I felt relieved. He dug every day. Occasionally he would eat something and smoke his pipe, but he didn't talk to me at all. There was no need to say anything. I was nothing more than a wandering, rootless ghost, and now, no longer the only absent member of our once five-member family, my presence was more bothersome than comforting. Now there were other dead he wanted to think about.

By the end of the fifth day, he had dug a pool large enough for all his grandchildren to swim freely. It took an additional three days to lay the stone and grout the entire bottom. Finally, he covered all of this with plastic tablecloths he had patched together. He put the hose into the pool and filled it with water. Two days later, he used a butterfly net to transfer the fish one by one into the pool. When I came to stand beside him I counted; there were forty-seven. He dumped several large tub-falls of chopped vegetables and fruit into the water, said a loud goodbye, and then forever freed his mind of them. Afterwards, he paid the workers their wages and permanently dismissed them, too. In the end, he came to me and said, "It's time to leave. You leave too. Go to Sohrab. Get as far away from here as possible. Go. Go higher." Once he'd said this, he picked up his suitcase, locked the house doors, got in his silver Buick Skylight, and disappeared in the twists and turns of the road leading to the city. But before leaving, he stuck his head out the car window and said one last thing: "And if you don't go, remember, I don't want you coming to see me. Beeta was right. We have to forge our own path and learn to live with the living."

CHAPTER 14

Ahh . . . The time had finally come . . . For the first time in my life I was all alone. I sat in my treehouse and thought about history and fate. I read books and thought about novels I'd dreamed of writing, while alive. I contemplated dreams I used to have but which now I could barely even remember. In addition to this, I enjoyed myself. I swam and played with Dad's grandchildren; climbed trees and ate greengage plums. I planted walnut, peach, and greengage saplings around the grove and allowed trees to take over, so that all was hidden from sight under their canopy. I spent time with birds and lizards and dragonflies, without trying to interpret them. Divination is just man's feeble attempt to comprehend an incomprehensible world.

With Dad gone, ghosts gradually started coming to visit. They came to chat with me about Razan's history, so the current situation would be easier to bear unaware that I liked my situation, had absolutely been waiting for it. When Dad told me to join Sohrab, I never considered actually listening to him. Now I was waiting, with all the time in the world. I wanted to stay until the return so I could answer the questions that would come. I knew there would be a return; and there would be questions about Beeta and Dad. I knew there would be a return; there would be also a visit to Sohrab's room to look through his papers and books and she would pick up *The Wayfarer* by Sohrab Sepehri and read it again, for the thousandth time. And so it was. Years later, when she hopped over the iron gate at the entrance to the grove with a speed and nimbleness that bore no resemblance to the woman she had been years before, I said to myself, "This woman is remarkable!" Signs of her age were visible in her hair, already grey from before, and her face was created by wrinkles both large and small, but she broke the lock on the door and entered the house with such self-assurance I thought, voilà the youngest living member of our family: Roza, my mother.

The days passed with monotonous regularity. Together with the other ghosts, I watched the people of Razan from up in my treehouse and I thought, we dead were all consistently happy, while each of the living was variously unhappy. It is not their unhappiness that is extraordinarily alluring and amazing for the dead, but rather the great variety of unhappinesses. Thousands of books could be written about this. Generations could discuss it millions of times over. I watched time from above as people repeated their days in ceaseless movement. The most futile thing in the world is counting. If this were not true, perhaps I would count the risings and setting of the sun and moon; the number of sunny, cloudy, and foggy days; the months and the seasons; and record them in my diary, just to kill time. Or maybe I would count the number of children born in the village during this time, or the baby foxes, jackals, rabbits, and hedgehogs that had been born in these last few years: how many had mated, bore young, and had died, right around my treehouse. Or maybe I would have passed the time by counting the days of my solitude, but I knew it was just chasing after the wind, as it is said in the Book of Ecclesiastes. Instead of counting objects and days and hours, if people would simply rub their palms together just once, and comprehend that mysterious skin-to-skin contact fully, their understanding of the world would be better. Or if just once they were to watch and understand the blooming of a flower or birth of a lamb, using their senses of sight and hearing and smell completely, perhaps humans would come to the conclusion that in all the days and nights of their lives, only that minute in which they are immersed is worth calculating. During those years of solitude and long periods of sleeplessness, I realized that I was obsessed with the moment a flower bursts into bloom.

Early in the morning before daybreak I would sit next to buds and watch the birth of a drop of dew. The reflection of the sunrise would appear within it, then the dew would evaporate, and I would hear the bud's soft sigh, uttered in a small space, in a lapse between the commotion of people and nature. I would touch the freshly opened petals with my fingertips; with all my sense of touch, I would feel them as petals; I would smell them and allow their fragrance to spread through me.

Gradually I learned to close my eyes and concentrate all of my six senses into my sense of hearing to better hear the flowers' sigh. Then I learned to distinguish the sigh of rosebud from that of a fig blossom. The opening rosebud emits a sigh like the gentle kiss of a shy beloved on her lover's lips, sweaty with love's intensity; but the blooming of a fig blossom is like a beloved's kiss given in the air to her distant lover. Like gossamer lips tenderly blowing a kiss into space.

During this time, I also learned that the most beautiful things are those that are least well known among humans. Just like the Japanese quince, which is rarely seen in gardens but has a flower of Japanese beauty and grace, and miniature curves. The kiss of a Japanese quince as it blooms is the most bashful of all. Just like the kiss of a barely pubescent girl in a peach-colored kimono who kisses her own thin, white arm hidden from the eyes of others, as she dreams about the lover she has never had, the touch she has never known, and the kiss she has never tasted. The kiss of a Japanese quince is the kiss of a virgin given to her own immaculate virginity.

It was thus that I let the years of solitude touch me,

resisting the temptation to visit Beeta, Dad, or Mom; instead, gazing at the grove and Razan in the leaden, soporific stillness. Razan, with its ancient secrets—a village whose beginning is unknown, or at least its oldest resident.

Although it seemed the memories of Razan's older generation were bound and knotted together with the *sabzeh* sprouts[35] and thus bequeathed to the river every year with the *haft-sin* of Nowruz[36], everyone was so preoccupied with remembering what they called "Razan's holy fire," that the memory of this was still vivid. At that time, everyone agreed that Homeyra Khatun's house was the oldest in the village and, although no one knew who was older than who, Issa and Effat's grandmother, Homeyra Khatun, imagined herself to be the oldest person in the village, while the village leader maintained he was the oldest; and at least five other people had the same claim. All of them thought themselves to be about one hundred and twenty-five. Before the teachers from the Literacy Corps set foot in Razan in the time of the Shah, nobody there knew about paper money, calendars, clocks, ID cards, or marriage certificates. They didn't even know that in a distant city there were people who travelled, not with horses and mules, but with wheeled contraptions made of metal; who didn't cultivate their food but bought it from shops.

In those years Razan was still so untouched that after three full days of getting lost and turning circles in their jeeps in the forest, hills, and dirt roads, the Literacy Corps was, eventually,

[35] Knotting sprouts is an ancient tradition that is practiced at the time of Nowruz, the Iranian New Year and first day of spring. The green blades that are grown by each family are tied together and wishes are made. It is believed that if the knot comes untied the wish will come true.

[36] A table that is laid out for *Nowruz*, the New Year, with seven symbolic items that all begin with the letter *sin*.

forced to capture some half-wild horses to guide them to Razan along animal paths in the forest. When the first teachers set foot there in 1964, the people didn't know what knives and forks were, or what such things as electricity or television could be. People had heard from their parents that the First Soothsayer's ancestor had been the only literate person in the village and had always carried around a book that he had called the History of Razan. It was for that reason, with the birth of a child, whatever book had been passed down in the family, be it the *Shahnameh,* Hafez, the *Avesta*, the *Masnavi, One Thousand and One Nights*, or *Amir Arsalan Namdar*, it would be taken to him to record the date of the child's birth on the inside cover.

Many long years had passed since then, and because of the Literacy Corps, some village children were eventually literate enough to read the birthdates of their forefathers in the ancestral books. It was then that they discovered that the First Soothsayer's great ancestor appeared not only to have had limited literacy himself, but of the three hundred and sixty-five days of every year, he only knew how to write one. When the now literate children of the village got together and compared all the ancestral books kept by their illiterate families to find the birthdates of their forefathers and grandparents, all of them were confronted with a single date: 12.12.1212.[37] With the revelation that several generations had been duped, an outrage erupted in the village that left the First Soothsayer blamed for everything, as though he had been responsible for his ancestor's doings.

At first the village children and then their families, and finally the Literacy Corps teachers, started speculating about the mysterious date. The teachers consulted the few history

---

[37] In the Gregorian calendar the equivalent is 03.03.1834.

books they had brought with them, but found nothing. Then the village elders gathered to discuss various propositions, but in the end all were left frustrated and despairing. Their forefathers had been fooled for more than a hundred years and, even worse, had given the First Soothsayer's ancestor more respect than he deserved because they had considered him to be the village's memory and written history. Then the village grandmothers and grandfathers recalled that the First Soothsayer's ancestor had had a manuscript book. After all the inconclusive research and speculation about 12.12.1212, they then raided the abandoned, run-down house that had belonged to the First Soothsayer's ancestor and searched the whole structure, even scouring the thorns and grasses and bushes that filled it, but found nothing. True, these revelations had led the people to despair, but from that day forward, Razan's history became important for everyone. Everyone wanted to know who their forefathers were, and whether they were related to the Zoroastrian ghosts in the area; why they had come here, what they had done; and the mystery of why the illiterate villagers still owned so many books. Could it be that their ancestors had been able to read and write?

The villagers turned their cupboards and dank attics inside out, pulling out two-hundred-year-old carved wooden trunks, but they found nothing except moth-eaten cloth, and the skeletons of lizards and mice. They gave the only books unspoiled to their now-literate children to search for any trace of their literate forefathers; but again, this led nowhere. And so, cupboard doors were closed again, attics were locked once more after a good cleaning and the setting of fresh mouse traps; and wooden trunks were stowed away in basements to, again, be relegated to history and forgotten with the rise of the sun after a month of frenzied effort to uncover the history of their ancestors. Gradually they consoled themselves by saying, "What's the use of history, anyway?" And anyway, they still had the "present," the most important thing anyone could have. One villager said, "The past is for the dead." Another said, "We'll write our own history from now on." And yet a third said, "If they had been respectable people, they surely would have passed some valuables down to us." It was thus that the people considered themselves, finally, absolved from any fault or ambiguity. They were exuberant, as though it were the first day of Creation and they were making or experiencing everything for the very first time; as though, suddenly, they were freed from the weight of their grandfathers' counsel and their grandmothers' moralizing tales and a thousand years of glorious history. A glory, even the tiniest trace of which, was no longer to be found.

And so, early that morning when the villagers made the unannounced decision to free themselves of the vices of their ancestors' legacy, the sun rose as never before. Radiant and fresh and clear, it hoisted itself above the low-lying fog and, rising from the plants like spirits imprisoned in the earth, vapor climbed into the sky to join the clouds. Suddenly, the air was fresh. Just like the first day of Creation when the earth was empty and shapeless and the Spirit of God commanded, "Let there be light!" as it moved upon a dark mass of vapor. And it became light, and God was pleased with the light, and He separated it from the darkness.

Foxes and jackals ran in oblivious bliss through the thick fog away from the chicken coops and rice paddies, taking refuge in their dens to dream all day about their nocturnal hunt for chickens and geese. As it did every morning, the cuckoo continued his eternal quest for his lover, loudly asking all creatures, "Coo? Coo? Coo? Coo?"[38] The village felt as if it had been reborn, everything fresh and new as if it had been

---

[38] In Persian *kū*, a shortened version of *kojā,* means 'where'.

transported back a hundred years; lovers were so bashful they couldn't exchange simple messages with their beloved, or even gaze long into one another's eyes. The world had again become so trustworthy that a single glance transported them to the precipice of madness and love. A single drunken glance from one who had spent a night in worshipful wakefulness was enough for the girl who saw it to know she was prepared to wait for that look for the rest of her life. Dowries became simple again like hundreds and thousands of years ago, no girl asked for *mahr*[39] or bridewealth, and no man enquired about dowries or virginity. In discovering there was no history, the people had returned to the Age of Innocence, wild greengage blossoms glistened and were fragrant just like on an early morning in the Garden of Eden. The river ran clear and full of fish, and the people were in awe of the interpretations of the dreams that seemed to have suddenly swept over them.

One villager dreamed that a woman with a burning torch came to see her, introducing herself as her ancestor and, pointing to the hill that had been part of our family grove for years, said she lived there and had come to wash her white robes in the villager's courtyard, for a funeral. No matter how much the villager asked, "Whose funeral? And why 'white'?" the woman replied dolefully, "If you're clever, perhaps one day you'll understand." The next day when the villager got up and went to wash her face in the well, as she did every morning, she saw white robes hanging on the line, fluttering in the wind. One man dreamed that an eighty-eight-year plague came and destroyed all of Razan, including the distant meadows and forests. It blackened the earth—making it sterile—and burnt the trees. A five-year-old child dreamed the family books were

---

[39] Money that has to be paid by the groom to the wife at the time of marriage.

burned in the square while a man in a black turban danced around the fire, laughing.

At first the dreams were full of warning and menace, then they gradually became pleasant. They became good dreams. They seemed to be informing the dreamers of the past and the future, while at the same time awash with needs and desires in the present. People who had been afraid to dream now wanted to so that the First Soothsayer could tell them what they meant. Before long, however, the dreams themselves had become so realistic, so like daily life, that interpreting them became meaningless. With the deletion of history and the onslaught of pleasurable dreams, the villagers gradually forgot about food and work and became frail plants that fed on oxygen. The frailer their bodies became, the more their minds grew—so much so that the images within collided and merged. After a time, they met one another in their dreams, ate together in their dreams, fell in love, and made love in their dreams.

Things continued like this for days and weeks until one day the First Soothsayer had a lucid dream in which he called everyone together and ordered them to wake up and return to their daily lives. But the people, who had never disregarded his instructions while awake, even recently with the honesty of his ancestor called into question, now ignored him completely. They couldn't break away from their dream life, a carefree life, free of suffering and responsibility. In the dreams, no one caused suffering to anyone else, and they weren't as hungry as they had been in their lives before the dreams began. They lived their desires while dreaming. If two people were in love with the same person, in their dreams they each lived happy lives with their lover without the presence of the other. If someone was poor, in their dreams they lived in a large house with crystal chandeliers, mirrored walls, and bathed every afternoon in a river of milk and honey; if someone couldn't get pregnant, in their dreams they were living happily together with their husband and children.

The First Soothsayer had wearied of the dreams that had suddenly inundated him and others, and had no choice but first to wake himself. Once he had managed to wake up, with magic, ancient incantations, and the help of supernatural forces in his dreams, he found the village in a static stupor. Time was standing still. He went to the door of every house and knocked to rouse its inhabitants, to tell them that if things continued in this way, they would all soon turn into dry, hollow plants that would splinter at the slightest touch. Yet no one stirred. No one at all.

Fighting to stay awake, the First Soothsayer went to the deserted house of his ancestor in the hope of finding a solution. He had been there in recent months, together with the villagers, to search for the History of Razan, but instinct told him that this time he would be able to find something, a recess, a clue, a solution. And so it was. After searching for three days and nights in the dirt and grime, beneath overgrown grasses and among legless lizard skeletons and skins, he found the book under a wooden board, in a metal box, in the basement. However, reading it wasn't as easy as he'd imagined. It was written in *abjad* numerals[40] and *shajara* and *jomal*.[41]

---

[40] A system by which the 28 letters of the Arabic alphabet are assigned numerical values. The name *abjad* comes from the first four letters in Semitic alphabets (A-B-J-D). One of its uses was in numerology, and it was also used in magic talismans and amulets.

[41] *Shajara*, a mystical script similar to *abjad* but where each letter of the Arabic alphabet is replaced by a letter with a vertical line from which varying numbers of perpendicular lines protrude at an angle resembling a tree. *Shajara* means tree in Arabic. *Shajara* was used like *abjad*; *jomal*, a way of calculating words written in *abjad* numerals that was sometimes used in talismans and treasure maps.

During the day as he checked on Razan's sleeping residents, separating the dead from the living and burying them, he began to learn *shajara* and *abjad* numerals. Eventually, after six weeks he was able to read the book and realized how mistaken the villagers had been about his ancestor.

As he deciphered the book, the Soothsayer understood that the great man, that great scholar of science and knowledge, knew the secrets of the plants and rocks. He could read the mystical scripts of centuries past, identify the invisible paths of the stars, and predict someone's fate upon seeing the palm of their hand. He was a man who had died multiple deaths, had been brought back to life, and, in the world, he had meandered between life and death. Thus he neither feared death nor was excited by life. He interpreted honest dreams, could see someone's previous lives by looking into their eyes, and reminded them of their duties in their current life. He was always alone but never spoke of loneliness. He was free but did not contemplate freedom. His life was bound by all those things that others didn't know but were prepared to give half their lives to understand. In his book he wrote: *Although it is commonly said that I am from Razan, I alone know that I simply appeared one day in the forest and when I stand in front of a mirror and look at the lines on my face and in my eyes, I can't see where I was before.* However, not trusting the fine, almost invisible lines of the iris of his eyes, he was sure he had lived many lives to have had access to such knowledge. Knowledge, higher than any other. Knowledge, that even in the distant past had long been forgotten, leaving not even so much as a name. Knowledge, far beyond *simiyya* and *limiyya*[42] and alchemy, and other occult sciences that now featured in every young boy's tongue-twisters.

---

[42] *Simiyya*, the occult science of reviving the dead; *limiyya*, the occult science of capturing jinns and spirits.

Reading quickly and with mounting excitement, the Soothsayer was so astounded by his ancestor's memoirs and knowledge that he forgot about Razan and its sleeping inhabitants until he reached several lines he couldn't fathom. The great scholar of sciences and knowledge had written about how the inhabitants of Razan had fallen into an enchanted sleep after forgetting the history of their village, and how, after breaking the charm, he had promised to write a history for future generations. He identified 12.12.1212 as the date the enchanted slumber was lifted. The date on which, thanks to him, the people were reborn. So, it wasn't for nothing that he had considered it the date of birth of every newborn. It was the date of awakening for the people of Razan.

Though consumed by the book, the Soothsayer thought his first duty would be to rescue the villagers from the enchanted sleep; and so, he had no choice but to resist the temptation to continue reading and head into the depths of the forest, with the book as his guide. He reached a large circular clearing. For three days and nights he sat in the center of the circle and fasted; and as he resisted the temptation to eat or sleep, he scourged the dusty recesses of his mind to, as the book instructed, *remember*. It was written: *In the mind of the seeker, the correct place, from the unworthy is concealed.* It was written: *The true seeker of Bushasp, the demon of deep sleep, is he who knows by word of mouth. He can find him with his inherent perception.* It was thus that after three days and nights of fasting and trance, he followed the flight path of the first firefly. He walked for days and nights in rain, fog, and moonlight until he was consumed by silence in an unknown part of the forest. He saw a plunging valley that was in half-darkness at high noon. No birds sang, no breeze rustled the trees, and not even a snake slithered through the dried leaves covering the ground. Everything had sunk into a lethargic stasis. He remembered that the book had referred to a "River of Oblivion." Straining his ears, he heard a single sound. It was the gentle, torpor-inducing flow of the River of Oblivion, one sip of which would wipe one's memory forever. The River of Oblivion that flowed past the abode of the sleeping demon. As he continued, he was filled with transparent fear. How frightening could the demon be and why was there no indication in the book of weapons with which to defend oneself? He continued with trepidation until he reached a cave where the intoxicating opium poppy and *haoma*[43] plants were growing. As he entered the cave, he saw an enormous old demon who had fallen into a deep sleep; two small horns were protruding from its forehead, and his head was resting between his two large, white wings. His beard and hair were so long they reached his shins, and he was lying on a black fur pelt. The closer the Soothsayer got to the creature and the more he looked at him, the less he feared. Finally, he was forced to admit that not all demons are evil. After twenty-four hours of waiting for the demon to wake up, and drinking several cups of anti-sleeping potion that he had prepared according to the book's instructions and that kept him awake, he looked at the small fountain of oblivion water in the center of the room. Oh, how he wanted to drink from it! But then, remembering the book's instructions, he suppressed the temptation. Then, looking at the walls of the cave, he saw clear but muddled, enigmatic images of human dreams blending, then separating. In one of them, he found a recurring dream of his own in which he was kissing a pretty-faced girl he had wanted to kiss for years.

In the end, he had no other choice but to break a twig off the *haoma* plant and stick it up the decrepit demon's nose. The enormous old demon awoke with a sneeze and then, looking at

---

[43] A plant which plays a role in Zoroastrian doctrine and Persian mythology. The *haoma* plant is thought to be a type of ephedra and had ritual applications when it was pressed and drunk.

him from under eyelids heavy with sleep, he calmly asked the Soothsayer what he wanted. The Soothsayer explained the problem of the dreams and asked the demon to leave his people alone so they could return to a normal life. The Demon of Sleep, unable even to recall which people and which village the Soothsayer was referring to, said, "I'm not the one who goes after people; it is always the people who come after me. Now, go back. This very night they will all have dreams such that they will no longer want to sleep during the day." No sooner had the demon spoken these words than he fell back into a deep sleep.

After three days and nights when the Soothsayer arrived at the village with a thousand worries that the demon may not have kept his word, he found it more full of activity than it had ever been. The people had no recollection of the days and weeks they had spent in slumber; all they knew was that they had all had a strange, indescribable dream. Each villager would start to recount their dream, then, stopping, would hurriedly add, "But that wasn't it. The feeling was much worse. I can't describe it." All of them were in the same dream and though devoid of clear images, they all awoke with headaches and nausea, and a sense of unease and distress. Upon realizing that those who had died were no longer with them, they suddenly also noticed that the chicken coops had been half-emptied by night-raiding foxes and jackals; that in their search for fresh grass, the cows and sheep had broken stall doors and were wandering in the forests, fields, and rice paddies, eating half of the green rice plants; spiders had spun their webs everywhere; creeping flowers and plants had entered their rooms; and beds smelt of death and sex and nightmare-induced sweat. So, when the First Soothsayer entered the village, happy yet exhausted from his long journey, everyone was so busy catching up on all their work that no one turned to look at him or make the effort to return his greetings.

CHAPTER 15

When Hushang turned the old key in the lock on the iron gate and heard the whine of its rusty hinges, he found himself looking at the same large, flower-filled yard, and the same ancient pine and buttonwood trees that had inhabited it since his birth. The dogwood trellis, and under it his mother, father, and old grandfather sat drinking saffron or sour cherry tea as they had every afternoon for as long as he could remember. They smiled over at him as if from an eternal framed photograph. After all the tragic, futile suffering and upheaval, he found himself once again face to face with a little piece of paradise. He was not surprised to see that scene again after so many years. They smiled at him as if from the picture's eternal script, as though for ages they had been waiting for him to insert his now-rusty key into the lock of their Qajar house, appear before them with disheveled grey hair, pale face, and desperate eyes, and ask, "Is there still room for me in this house?"

Nobody asked questions. Not his mother, Gordafarid, nor his father, Jamshid, and not even his grandfather, Manuchehr. They let him drift for days from room to room, from terrace to sitting room, from living room to storage room, from library to basement. He didn't even know what he was looking for. He opened cupboard doors and stood staring at their contents, feeling them just like a curious and aimless little boy, or staring at their mysterious emptiness. He went to the attic and basement, opening the locks on ancient suitcases and chests, and spending hours fiddling with the old, dusty objects within. He gazed at them as if they were speaking to him beyond language and history, telling him tales of their fate in his absence. He touched old statues, Qajar paintings, paintings by Kamaleddin Behzad, and calligraphy by Mir Emad. He moved handwoven silk carpets aside and, remembering the silkworms he raised in Razan, carefully inspected their corners and knots.

He spent hours locked in the library without reading a single page; he flipped through books, smelt them. He examined notes written in the margins and tried to guess or remember which handwriting was his own, which was Khosrow's, and which belonged to his father and grandfather. He looked at the book stamps, at the large notebook with an alphabetic catalogue by subject of all the books, at their classification, written years ago in his and Khosrow's hand. Every book he touched was more than a book. It was a memory. His entire destiny. It was longing.

He recalled how years ago—so long ago he couldn't even remember what he looked like at the time—he and Khosrow had spent days arranging all five thousand seven hundred and thirty-two books in alphabetical order and classified them according to subject. Oh, how they had enjoyed this! He remembered how they first thought it would only take them a week to finish, but by the end of that first day they realized how wrong they were. As if it were possible to pick up a book and simply write the classification numbers and letters on its cover and then send it off to a bookshelf! Once they had a book in hand, who knew when they would put it down again? They skimmed through them, allowing passages to catch them like fishing nets and carry them down into the depths of their sea. They would read sections aloud and discuss them. Then suddenly they would realise that hours had passed and all the books were still strewn around them on the floor; the dinner their mother, Gordafarid, had brought had gone cold, and they were still sunk in books they had picked up that morning. Even after his father and grandfather came to help them, the situation didn't much improve, the difference being that now four people were lost in reading. They discussed books they had in hand, argued, wrote notes in the margins, and then had no choice but to temporarily abandon them to continue the classification.

A faint smile played on his lips as he turned and smelt pages in the uncensored family library, recalling that that hadn't even been the half of it. As they worked on the classification, each of them also went—as was tradition—to buy books once a week from the bookstores on Naser Khosrow, and later Enghelab Street; and if it hadn't been for Gordafarid's timely scolding, who knows when the work would have been completed. But four months later, the library was organized in a way befitting of it. A desk was placed along each of the four walls, and a six-person Italian furniture set sat upon Qajar-era carpets from Kashan so there would be a place to rest. Yes, it is true, the first and last of the family's hereditary manias was a mania for reading.

Now after all these years, as he wandered back and forth enraptured by memories of his youth, Dad missed Khosrow more than ever. They hadn't lived together for years, but so much of their happy childhood, youth, and young adulthood had been spent exchanging thoughts and experiences; nobody could ever have imagined that life would subsequently keep them so far apart.

Continuing with an almost childlike curiosity, Dad went to the kitchen, examined the old ceramic dishes and copper pots, then used them to make himself a fried egg. He stood for hours behind the stained-glass windows watching the tiny flecks of dust suspended mid-air in the colored shafts of sunlight. Perhaps he was looking for his childhood, or years lost and forgotten spent in that multi-storied, eighteen-bedroom house with its vestibules, pointed barrel vaults and colored sash windows. Perhaps he was still following the mysterious fragrance of his beloved Roza's body and the memory of the very first time her presence graced its corridors.

After days of a kind of malaise, he finally made a decision, and found his centre of gravity: a place that had remained as untouched as all the house's walls and carpets and colored windows. A place that had remained safe from the invasion of savage forces outside: the library; the old, large, uncensored library.

Despite this and even with all of his silence, Dad's return to his father's house brought with it a sense of youthful excitement. Those who became youthful were Gordafarid, Jamshid, and Manuchehr. They got up before dawn. Jamshid went to the bakery, Manuchehr put on a record of Badizadeh, opened the windows, and sprayed water on the courtyard, while Gordafarid started getting things ready for breakfast. When the fragrance of tea and fresh *sangak* bread[44] was wafting through the house, they woke the young one in their midst—though now an old man with grey hair—and let the sound of Badizadeh penetrate the fibres of his being. They spread the tablecloth on the floor, on the Qajar-era carpets, or on the platform in the courtyard, and by the time they were all seated and had sweetened their tea, the sounds of their soft "Good mornings" spread a sense of gaiety throughout the house and garden. Enchanted by the scent of jasmine and four o'clock flowers, Hushang began to talk, to forget the few happy days he had spent in Razan. He spoke about the nice weather, about the changes he saw in Tehran, about concerns with losing the family home to the mayor. But not about Razan, no! Not about Roza, or Beeta, Sohrab, or me. Never!

---

[44] A type of Iranian bread cooked on small hot stones.

Grandma and Granddad explained that the mayor had personally come to their house and garden under various pretexts to express his interest in purchasing it, but eventually gave up trying to bribe them, which was when the intimidation began. First, they threw Khosrow into prison for his mystical beliefs. But even though he knew what it was really all about, Khosrow refused to meet with the mayor to tell him to cease his games. It was thus that the mayor found himself again without ammunition. He didn't give up, however, instead seeking revenge by at least sponsoring measures to have the house demolished. A proposal for a new highway was approved together with a demolition order for their home; so, for months, the bulldozers had been ready to come and flatten the trees and that beautiful Qajar house, out of spite. The thing is, despite such terrible threats, neither Grandma or Granddad were angry or depressed, nor was Great Granddad Manuchehr, who had lived longer than even the trees in the courtyard. When Dad asked them anxiously what they were going to do, Granddad simply replied, "I don't care what he does, we're not budging," finishing the sweetened tea he was drinking in a single gulp.

And it was thus that Dad gradually found his place in the house. He had such a thirst for reading that he didn't care if it was Sophocles or Bertrand Russell. The only thing that mattered was that he connected with the world's thinkers and thus ensured his distance from the contemporary world of intellectual midgets that had overrun the country. He wanted to elevate his mind again. Over time, he structured his studies. For a while he read ancient plays, then Iranian and Mesopotamian mythology, then tomes on ancient religions. Later, he read political theory, sociology, and ideological thought; and the role of religions in war, and human being's intellectual rigidity. He read books about the Arab invasion of Iran and the reasons for the collapse of the Sassanian Empire, and compared them with the reasons for the fall of the Shah and the foundation of the Islamic Republic. He remembered many things he had known and read before his books were burned, but which seemed themselves to have fallen victim to fire. It was then he realized that sorrow brings oblivion.

Eventually, Hushang reached contemporary Iranian history; the place where all his questions turned into bottomless chasms. He bought the newspaper every day, and though he knew that much of it was devoid of truth, he wanted to know what had become of the rest of the population while he had been away—after the war, after the mass executions, after the flight of the educated and wealthy from the country. He still didn't have the courage to leave the house, to walk among people in the streets who, either through their silence or their ignorance, had practically killed others to take their places. He still couldn't forgive: not others, and not himself.

When Nietzsche was writing *Beyond Good and Evil*, I'm sure the last thing he thought was that one day, it would result in the spiritual reconciliation of two brothers. Perhaps if Hushang hadn't picked up the book that day, he would never have had the chance to take Khosrow into his arms and relive his childhood with him. Khosrow appeared in the room muttering to himself, "There's not a single person who knows what is good and what is evil!" Standing there, his body now half transparent so great was his spiritual ascent, puffing on his hand-rolled bidi cigarette and blowing its fragrant smoke into the air, he said firmly, "Yet the line between the two has always been clear."

Of course, Hushang was not surprised by Khosrow's diminished opacity. These types of things always happened. That was why he began the endless discussion with his brother that would be continued in books beyond his own lifetime. It was a discussion that illustrated how differently they thought, and yet taught them just how close they still were despite the distance and differences, and how much they had missed each other over all these years. By the end of the day, after their *ghormeh sabzi* got cold twice and was no longer edible, they were still discussing their experiences and thoughts so passionately that in the end they embraced and kissed, their eyes wet with childlike ecstasy.

The next morning, though, Dad continued studying alone. He still wanted to know how the Iranian culture and civilization, with all its grandeur and creativity, with its belief in good thoughts, good words, and good deeds, had collapsed and reached such depths. Uncle Khosrow, on the other hand, truly did not want to know anything. He just wanted to float like an innocent being in a stream of cosmic consciousness and utter acceptance, and occasionally appear in a library somewhere in the world to read a book.

At first it angered Dad to see that all Khosrow did in the face of the monumental social and familial injustice was to appear and disappear in absolute stillness and serenity from home to library to ancient temple high in the Himalayas; not even caring to watch Iranian television or listen to international radio. Dad thought, *Doesn't he see all the killings, unemployment, depression, the lack of prospects, and the disillusioned people?* Put simply, Dad was angry. Angry with himself, angry with society, and with the world; and he dumped all his unanswered questions on his brother. But just as he was about to bombard him with questions, his eyes fell on the soft, clear lines on Khosrow's face as he sat with childlike serenity in meditation under a buttonwood tree in the corner of the courtyard. He thought he should take more time to understand his younger brother. A brother whom he knew all these years had been a seeker. He knew he'd spent years in India, Tibet, and Siberia learning from shamans, mystics, and ascetics. He knew his brother could read mysterious ancient scripts and possessed manuscripts that had the spiritual and material value of entire museums. He knew he had been through his share of hardships; he had been to prison, and, years ago, his wife had cheated on him and fled with a wealthy woman to France, where the fight for gay rights had just begun. He knew Khosrow's failure in love had dealt him such a blow that, forever after, he'd shied away from the ties of a serious relationship, although in India he once fell desperately in love with a female mystic who had devoted herself to a rat temple. He knew he had travelled endlessly, taken unknown, endless roads that led to other unknown, endless roads. He read books and meditated just enough to become astute in human relationships.

Instead of reprimanding his brother, Hushang thought it better to take a look inward and ask himself what *he* had done all these years. A heady question with a depressing answer. It was thus that he locked himself in his study room away from Khosrow and the others and began to berate himself. What had he done save letting all those catastrophes crumble down upon himself and his family? In moving to Razan then returning to Tehran, hadn't he just run away from the uncontrollable bitterness of his life? He concluded that much of what influences our lives happens in our absence. He concluded that if he hadn't given up and run away to Razan when the Revolution started and I was killed, but instead had tried to start and guide even a small movement with like-minded people, at least he would have felt better about himself now. Then he thought about Mohammad Mokhtari[45], Parvaneh and Dariush

---

[45] A leftist poet and writer who was assassinated in the serial assassinations of the 1990s, carried out by the Ministry of Intelligence against those who were ideologically opposed to the government. This string of murders left more than eighty people dead.

[46] A husband and wife couple who led the Mellat-e Iran Party and were assassinated in their home by members of the Ministry of Intelligence.

[47] A researcher and writer, and another victim of the serial assassinations.

Forouhar[46], and Mohammad Pouyandeh[47]. He thought about executed bloggers and social activists who had just appeared in an article or the news, after years of silence. Despite all the strict censorship implemented by the Ministries of Islamic Guidance and Intelligence, you could still find informed critical commentary about the state of Iranian society in some books and, here and there, in literary and social science publications. He thought, *It seems society is still alive. It's breathing. It's reacting to excess.* If he'd been like them, if he'd worked and at least formed a music group instead of leaving behind music altogether, would he not have contributed what he could to society? If he had not stayed his fiery tongue it would surely have cost him his life. What then would have become of Roza? Oh Roza . . . Roza . . . Roza . . . Where are you?!

The next time Khosrow came to visit Dad was the worst possible time. That morning, Dad was beside himself with fury after reading about the disappearance of several politically active university students, the disappearance of twenty thousand pages from a criminal file, and a corrupt judge presiding over a murder case. His rage was just waiting to explode. And so, when Dad saw the book Khosrow was holding, he completely lost his temper, snarling at his brother, "What good is this mystical bullshit in the real world?" Taken aback by the question and tone, Khosrow didn't say anything. *The Golden Future* by Osho was open in his hands. He closed it calmly, sat down, and looked hard at Dad, waiting till his anger had cooled. Seeing his silence, Dad became even more heated and said in a louder voice, "When my Sohrab was executed for no reason, when they burned my daughter, and when my wife lost her mind and left, what help was your mystical bullshit then?" Deeply saddened again by these tragedies, Khosrow remained silent.

Dad continued, "When all those innocent political prisoners

were executed, when all those young men were killed in a delusory war, when all those rights were revoked, what good did this mysticism game of yours do?" Khosrow sighed, let his head fall to his chest and said reproachfully, "Truly nothing!"

Dad's voice rose to a yell, "The world is consumed by murder, injustice, and suffering and smart people like you go and hide in the safety of temples instead of doing something to fight the corruption and injustice!" And then suddenly his shoulders shook, and he began to sob loudly. Years of smothered tears poured out of him, soaking the books and carpets. As warm tears flowed down his cheeks, onto his shirt, all he wanted was to drown in a river of his own tears and die. He couldn't see any reason to continue living. Everything that he once loved with all his heart had been taken from him in the worst possible way. His *tars*, his home in Tehran, Roza, Sohrab, Beeta, me, and worst of all, our aspirations. And they were even going to destroy this Qajar house which has documents to prove it had belonged to the family for two hundred years. What more could they possibly want? Sitting there, tears rolling down his cheeks, his head sunk onto his arms, he wished he had just been buried by the black snow.

Khosrow wanted to get up and take his brother's hunched shoulders in his arms, and apologize for the fact that mysticism didn't offer any simple solutions to murder, plunder, poverty, or human injustice. But instead he paused, then left the room so Dad could cry in peace. Just before leaving he stopped a moment as he walked past Dad and squeezed his brother's shoulder.

That night when he let himself into the library again, he saw Dad leaning against a chair reading as usual. It was only then that he allowed himself to sit down in his usual chair and say, quietly, "Most people see the world as a dangerous and threatening place they have to arm themselves against, fight with, protect themselves or run away from. And for these people the world truly becomes a menacing, harmful, aggressive creature. But the world is something one needs a lifetime just to know."

Seeing that Dad was still silent, he shook his head, remorsefully, and continued, "You say that the world has become crazy and ask what can I do for it. My answer is this: all I can do is not get caught up in the madness." Uncle Khosrow went on, "You can only know swimming by swimming, love by loving and meditation by meditating. There's no other way. The mind opens outward and meditation inward. That's the difference between your world and mine."

He looked uncertainly at Dad, unsure if he was still listening or not, and cautiously continued, "I don't blame you. Time is in transition and everything we loved is being destroyed. Look around you. These books, these manuscripts, this calligraphy; illumination, architecture, landscaping; these miniatures—they don't exist anywhere anymore. Instead of these carpets with meaningful thousand-year-old motifs they sell factory-made rugs featuring Mickey Mouse; and instead of one telephone occasionally ringing from a corner of every house, every five-year-old has a mobile phone. All the old gardens, historical houses, ancient artifacts, handicrafts, national treasures, and everything else that was a product of thousands of years of Iranian civilization, and culture and thought, has been destroyed or is today in the process of being destroyed and looted. In this savage onslaught, where people have lost their identity and their past, leaving them alienated from each other, do you think there's anyone who, alone, can do something? Perhaps the only solution would be a united mass movement, but where is the unity in these people? We need unity to destroy, and unity to construct." He paused, then went on, "With all this destruction, all I can do is not become tainted by something I don't believe in. Alas, if only I could do more!" Dad didn't look up from his book—as though he hadn't heard—perhaps because, although he understood, he couldn't console himself with Khosrow's words. His whole being was bursting with the suffering that a swayed society had unleashed. Reading history books and listening to the news didn't lessen all the pain and rage within, but just added to it. He felt desperate and distressed. He loathed cruelty, war, and injustice; at the same time, he couldn't comprehend the silence in the face of it all. Like an unknown quote whispering over and over in his ear he heard: *future generations will ask themselves why they were obliged to spend their lives in darkness after morning had dawned once again*. But what he said was, "Tomorrow I'm going out."

The next day he went out. Pulling on an ironed shirt and pair of slacks, he stood for a while in front of the mirror deliberating whether or not to put on a tie, eventually deciding to put one on. A navy-blue tie with a white shirt and a pair of black dress pants. He slowly opened the rusty courtyard door and, standing in its frame, he looked left and right down the street, unaware that his parents and grandfather were witnesses to his hesitation, each from behind a different window. In all the years since fleeing Tehran, he had only set foot there several times out of necessity, and he had always avoided walking around outside in the city. Even after selling the antiquities when he wanted to replenish his library after the mullah had looted and burned his books, he didn't go to Enghelab Street. Instead, he bought books from private libraries that had been advertised in the newspaper, and took them back to Razan.

Today, now for the first time, several decades after the Islamic Revolution, he wanted to go out into the streets and see the city: the people, the new roads, alleys, new stores with neon lights, and fast-walking women in black *mantos*, *manghe'es* and headscarves. He wanted to get a closer look at the new apartment blocks he had been told were built where once old gardens had flourished. He wanted to see the types of creatures

Tehran and its inhabitants had now become. He thought to himself, *I don't want to reconcile with these people and the thousand-headed viper of a regime. I just want to see what's left of society's battered corpse.*

Walking towards Tajrish Square, he tried not to stare at the people but look, instead, at the buildings and streets. After several hundred metres, he felt his body contract and the veins in his neck swell. He consoled himself by saying he was now an old man. Then he tried to ease his fear of people; people who not so long ago had so savagely burnt his daughter, his *tars* and his home.

The further along he walked, the more crowded the streets and stores became. He couldn't remember how many decades had passed since he'd gone to Shahanshahi Park, now called Mellat. There were big billboards, boutiques large and small with foreign clothing, iron railings lining the footpaths, large, double-length buses, tooting horns, and taxi drivers calling out to people on the footpaths. "Ma'am! Resalat?" "Sir! Sayed Khandan?"

He was feeling tired, but was determined to walk down to Shah Reza Street, now Enghelab. The city appeared calm as though there were no longer any atrocities or crimes taking place, quietly locked away behind prison doors. Walking towards him was a young couple holding hands. However, as the young man cast a sideways glance at the street, they let go abruptly and went pale. Dad followed their gaze. A green Patrol with the words "Morality Police" was driving past. Inside sat two chador-clad women and two men in military uniforms, driving slowly along the side of the street, carefully inspecting pedestrians. Once the Morality Police had passed, the couple began holding hands again. Dad looked at their faces as they got nearer. It seemed as though their reaction to the Morality Police had been the most normal thing imaginable; more normal than fear or surrender. This upset him greatly, and again a wave of negative thoughts flooded his mind. He had reached Pahlavi intersection, now called Valiasr. When several people bumped into him and continued without apologizing, he felt alien in his own country, as if nowhere was his home. He was not at ease in Razan, and in Tehran he was a stranger. He harangued himself for not seeing the positive things; there was still the University of Tehran, the City Theatre; there were buttonwood trees and ravens, and despite the suffocating atmosphere of terror, there were people who still held hands away from "their" eyes, as if to say, "Don't worry, my love! These difficult times will pass."

He was walking from the University of Tehran toward Esfand 24th Square—now called Enghelab—when, from a distance, he caught sight of a group of people dressed in black. Yesterday in the news he hadn't heard about any demonstration; if he had, he would never have ventured out. Worried, he decided to turn around but noticed that people continued to walk in the opposite direction, oblivious of the gathering. He went several steps, but he despised himself. He was embarrassed by his fear and worry and hate. If seventy-five million people could witness demonstrations, poverty, corruption, public executions, and arrests on a daily basis, why couldn't he? If Beeta was able to live with these people and empathize with them, why shouldn't he? *Of all these people walking towards Esfand 24th, surely I'm not the only one who has suffered. My children were, of course, not the only ones killed*, he thought to himself. He recalled reading recently that fifteen thousand people were killed for their political beliefs in the 1980s, alone. Therefore, there were others, too. Others who continue to survive, struggling between sorrow and joy, hope and despair. Perhaps with hope. Hope for change. Fundamental change.

He looked down at his feet. They were still retreating.

Moving him away from the group of people dressed in black. A very beautiful, lone, rose bush on the side of the road caught his eye; a defenceless rose bush; innocently alien, all alone in all that noise and smoke, the blackness and grey. All these years he'd sought beauty: beauty that had yet to be born, and beauty that had passed away a hundred years ago. He recalled how dazed and frightened he had been, fleeing the assault of new revolutionaries, fleeing Tehran. His search for beauty and tranquility had led him to Razan; but it wasn't long before "they" also arrived. *It didn't matter how far you ran. They would always find you in the end, and pull you down with them*, he thought. Now he found himself in Tehran once again. Still on the run. As his feet were taking slow, steady steps in flight, he lifted his head to look at people's faces all around; at passersby, at street vendors, at booksellers. He looked at drug addicts asleep in corners of old buildings and at people who, hunched over but with rapid steps, were coming and going without even taking notice of the group in black, as though each was living on his own planet.

He thought Tehran was also like an addict. A city addicted to smoke, to humiliation, to poverty and torpor whose slightest effort to sober up gave rise to panic. Tehran was an addict that wanted to get clean but lacked the will, and after several days of sobriety would begin using again with even greater intensity. It was an addiction to oppression, an addiction to poverty, and an addiction to inhibition and nostalgia.

As he fled further from the crowd in black, he thought of years past; years that came to be known as the Student Movement of 1999 and the Green Movement of 2009, which he had only read about in the paper and heard about from Beeta. Although those who helped perpetuate the Revolution and the war may not want to admit it, he thought to himself, the political movements that arose every few years after the war and came to be known as the Periods of Construction, Reform, Prudence, and the Return to the Golden Age of the Islamic Revolution, etcetera, though nothing more than a means to stabilize and entrench the regime's power, had all in fact been born of small revolts against the government. He realized that this regime was able to incorporate every revolt against it into the regime itself.

Again, he looked at his feet. They were still carrying him in the opposite direction. He had to do something. Somehow, he had to stop himself from fleeing. He paused in front of a music store. Entering for no reason, he looked at the rows of CDs. He didn't know what he was doing there, but he needed time to make the right decision. Finally, he turned to the shop assistant and said, "I haven't been here for ages. I'm looking for a unique singer: someone with a good voice and good music who has something new to say."

Glancing around at the other customers to make sure there was no one who looked suspicious, the young sales assistant reached under the counter and pulled out two CDs. "Homay and Mohsen Namjoo," he said, then added, "But of course there are others, too." Up until now, Dad's hands had been in his pockets—as if to keep them untainted by the city's sins. Now, he pulled them out and touched the two CDs hesitantly. He asked if he could listen to some songs on them. The sales assistant indicated that Dad should join him in the back room where he inserted Namjoo's CD into a stereo.

Ours is the pirated copy of the Godfather
Ours is the ashamed government
Ours is the inflated file
Ours is the loser wearing the national colors
Ours is the constructive criticism
So perhaps ours will be the future.

Dad was delighted with the bitter satire. Then the sales assistant put on part of one of Homay's songs.

What kind of world is this where drinking wine is wrong?
What kind of heaven is this where eating wheat is wrong?[48]
Tell the truth, tell the truth, the truth
Where is your lofty Paradise?
By the way,
There too is everyone and the ignoble one God?

Dad's eyes twinkled with joy. *Yes! They are still alive and reacting,* he thought, and asked, "Are women singing, too?" "Yes, they are," the young sales assistant assured him. "And very well, too, but underground." Then he pulled out two more CDs of secret concerts and handed them to Dad. Dad eagerly purchased all four of them, and thanking the young man, he left. He had made up his mind: he was going back to Enghelab Square. Carrying the four CDs in a small plastic bag, he took long strides back towards the group in black. The closer he got, the less he feared. The demonstrators were thrusting their fists into the air and chanting, just like at the beginning of the Revolution. But these fists weren't like those fists—those fists were firm and powerful, with the confidence of people who could easily kill, out of conviction, or at least betray or imprison a neighbor, a colleague or even their own children to be executed. These fists, in contrast, were bowed and limp, as if raised out of a sense of duty. There was no confidence or ideology behind these fists. These fists were being paid peanuts. A trivial attempt to consolidate a small corner of the wretched, narrow, abject power.

Despite their small numbers, the demonstrators had

---

[48] A reference to an episode in the Quran in which Eve is cast out of Paradise for eating a head of wheat.

214 · SHOKOOFEH AZAR

blocked the main road and stopped the flow of traffic. One hundred people at most. Everyone else was standing on the footpath either talking quietly among themselves, or standing, hands tucked under their armpits in an unconscious effort to maintain an inner distance, silently watching the listless, black-clad crowd. He stopped, too. He thought that his tie and ironed, white shirt made him stand out but didn't care. One demonstrator, reading from a piece of paper, chanted, "Death to England!" Then the rest of the crowd, mostly old men or youngsters with sparse beards, repeated after him, "Death to England!" Dad stood off to one side until he finally mustered the courage to ask someone standing nearby, "What's the occasion?" The middle-aged owner of a nearby bookstore answered, "Apparently, they're protesting against a caricature of the Leader that was drawn in England." Then he gave a smirk and added, "Every once in a while, these baby Hezbollahis find an excuse to show off."

The demonstrators' listless chanting continued until suddenly, several people started shouting. A group of men wearing shrouds[49] on which was written, *I obey you, o Khamene'i. I melt in Your rule, my life a sacrifice to the Leader*, and holding large posters of Ali Khamene'i, got out of several white Paykan sedans. Together with some angry and excited mullahs, they moved to the front of the protesters. Their faces were swollen with rage as they roared and beat themselves over the head, chanting, "Death to those against the Supreme Leader! . . . Death to England's slave! . . . Death to America's slave!" And, "Obedience to the Leader guarantees our victory!"

The crowd of people on the footpaths watching them had

---

[49] The 'shroud wearers' are an extremist, violent group that formed following the Revolutions. Its members are willing to kill and be killed for the good of the Regime. The wearing of a burial shroud is a reference to this willingness to be killed at that very moment.

become denser. Several shopkeepers anxiously began to pull down the metal shutters on their shops. The atmosphere had become very volatile. The middle-aged man whispered to Dad, "These guys are dangerous. It's best we go inside." But at that very moment, the eyes of one of the shrouded men fell on Dad's tie. He lunged forward wildly and hurled himself at Dad, yanking on his tie, yelling with his face so close to Dad's that he was sprayed in spittle. "You put on a tie to show you're a slave to Britain, did you? Ties belong to asses! To spies! Get the spy!" The words hadn't even fully left his mouth before three others assaulted Dad. He couldn't believe how fast it had all happened. The people in the sheets surrounded him, pushing him, spraying him with their spittle, and pulling him towards them, screaming, "Spy! . . . It's these guys who are threatening the Revolution! . . . Get him! . . . Take him!"

Several people on the footpath tried to intervene, and the bookseller took him firmly by the hand and yelled at the abusers, "You should be ashamed of yourselves! What has this man done? Leave him alone!"

However, this gave the bombastic gang the excuse they'd been waiting for to show off and spread fear. They grabbed both of them, shoved them in the car and carted them off. Once the passersby and spectators realized what had happened, they quickly disappeared into stores and alleyways. In the car, a gang member removed his shroud, violently ripped it in two, then used it to blindfold them. Both were terrified, and the bookseller, whose voice had previously been strong, now said with fear and pleading, "But sir, what did we do? We didn't even say anything!"

A voice yelled, "Shut up! Your fuck-up was defending a lover of the West."

"Gentlemen, I don't even know this man," Dad spoke up. "Let him go. He didn't do anything wrong."

Again, the cacophony of voices yelling and cursing, accompanied by slaps and punches directed at the two continued until the vehicle braked violently. A door opened and the bookseller was booted out. One of their abusers thrust his head out of the window and screamed, "Get lost, you piece of shit! Let this be the last time you open your mouth like that!"

As the car sped away, Dad was relieved that at least they'd released the bookseller. Then he felt the plastic bag being yanked from his hands. "Well, well, well! What do we have here? Didn't I say he was a spy? You listen to banned music!"

"I bought them right there in Enghelab Street," Dad said. "From an authorized store with a permit from your Ministry of Islamic Guidance."

Scornfully, the man replied, "And you can get rat poison at the pharmacy, sir, so why don't you buy some of that and take it!"

Dad didn't know how to respond to this kind of blind logic. The vehicle continued driving slowly through the alleys. After a moment, another voice that hadn't yet fully deepened said with unnerving softness, "Sir, all these years since the Revolution, all those people martyred for the country who fought and were killed; and in the end, you still put on a tie like that accursed Shah, and listen to these kinds of CDs?"

With a calm he didn't know he possessed, Dad said, "Which Revolution, war, and martyrs are you referring to? One that you didn't even see with your own eyes? You weren't even born."

The other responded with unexpected vehemence, "So you're insolent too! Tell me what country you've been in until now?"

For a second, Dad thought about lying and just naming a country in the hope that they would leave him alone, but then he remembered he didn't even have a passport to prove it. So he said, "This country!" One of them said, "So you're a royalist and you're spreading anti-government propaganda. Which of their gangs are you associated with?"

Dad said nothing. He tilted his head up to look out from

beneath the blindfold. Two soldiers had rushed to open and close the doors from the inside of an underground car park of an ordinary apartment building they had now entered. They lead him up several floors, pushed him into a hallway, and finally sat him down on a chair in a room. Then they tied his hands from behind and untied his blindfold. The room was dark. Several minutes later, the door opened and a weak light came on above him. The CDs he had bought were on a table in front of him. Before seeing the man, he heard his voice bellow at someone. "Who tied this man's hands? Untie them. Hurry up!" The door opened and someone untied his hands, and then left. A middle-aged man with a shadow of a beard and shirtsleeves rolled up above his elbows sat down opposite him. On his forehead, a dark, circular, brand-like mark was clearly visible. Dad knew that in the years after the Revolution, it had become popular for Hezbollahis to brand themselves with a hot spoon to show their membership and power; and to give the impression of great piety as if they ground their foreheads so hard into the *turbah* during prayer the skin had become calloused. Everyone said, and images in newspapers and on television proved, that anyone with any kind of position in this regime had three things in common: prayer beads in the hand, a mullah collar around the neck, and the mark of a hot spoon on the forehead.

The man began examining the CDs. Then, placing a piece of paper and a blue Bic pen in front of him, he said, "Write!"

"What should I write?"

The man said, "Whatever you remember!"

"Someone of my age remembers a lot of things," Dad retorted. "So much that it goes well beyond your patience and your large, lumbering system!"

The man's scowl deepening, he said, "I see that you have information about our system. Write about that then."

"That doesn't require any special information," Dad

snorted. "Every child, from the moment they enter school, finds your system forced upon them."

"What do you mean by that?" the man asked.

"You've set up a base of Twenty-Million Basij in every school and far away village. With the mosque, and Islamic Society."

"I see you don't believe in God either," the man exclaimed. "Do you know what the punishment for that is? Death! You are a Corrupter on Earth."[50]

Dad had never felt so serene. He gave a smirk, pushed the pen and paper back across the table towards the man and said, "So my crime and sentence are already clear. It's not worth the effort to write anything."

The man leapt to his feet angrily and flung his chair into a corner. "You apparently don't get it!" he screamed. "In half an hour this paper had better be full!" He walked towards the door taking the CDs with him. Suddenly the muscles in his face changed. He gave a chilling smile, and before slamming the door behind him, he said, "Write whatever your nostalgic heart desires . . ."

Dad glanced around the room. There was just the wall with the wooden door behind him. He looked at the pen and paper. Smiling, he thought to himself he'd been wanting to write his memoirs for years. No more than a few minutes had passed when he called, "Paper, please." Immediately someone—as though listening by the door—brought him several sheets. An hour later, he again said loudly, "Paper, please." The same soldier behind the door brought him a handful of paper. Two hours later he said yet again, "Paper, please. More! And a bit of water!" This time the incredulous soldier brought him an

---

[50] An expression from the Quran and Islamic legal jurisprudence used to designate people deemed a danger to society. The punishment for such individuals is death.

unopened ream of A4 paper and set it on the table together with a pitcher of water and large plastic cup.

Before leaving he cast a look at the stack of pages Dad had written and, as though feeling sorry for Dad's naivety, he shook his head despairingly as if to say, "Poor thing. Little do you know, with every line you write you give them more fuel for interrogation!"

But Dad seemed to have something else on his mind. Otherworldly things, more important than his own life: his history and that of his family; the whole history of Tehran and Razan—what else did he have to lose? He loosened his tie, then unbuttoned his shirt cuffs and rolled up his sleeves. He had no perception of time passing. He wrote and wrote until he fell asleep. Early the next morning he awoke to the sound of the interrogator sitting across from him and reading the pages. "So, your son was executed, your daughter burned to death, and your wife ran away!" the interrogator said.

Dad said nothing. He had a bad taste in his mouth. He was about to drink the last of the water left in the cup when the interrogator swiped the cup off the table, splashing Dad's face and clothes. "With the way you're playing around it's clear you haven't been beaten by Sepah intelligence sticks!" the interrogator yelled.

Still Dad said nothing. The man yelled even louder, "You're just making stories up? Your sister turned into a jinn and your daughter into a mermaid, and before going into the sea she gave birth to fish and shells?! There was black snow and Zoroastrian ghosts prayed for you?! A ghost showed you a treasure map?!" He let out a loud, nervous laugh. Then suddenly he jumped to his feet, and leaning with his hands on the table he bellowed, "With your grey hair and those wrinkles of yours I thought you must be someone respectable with something respectable to say, but now I see you just dreamt up some children's stories. Especially the part about the ghost of your dead daughter living with you! Hahahaha! . . . You should be in the loony bin, not here!"

Turning to the door he yelled, "Soldier!" A soldier entered with a salute. Squinting, the interrogator brought his face close to Dad's and said, "I was planning to let you go quickly because yesterday they just wanted to make a scene by pulling you out of the crowd and bringing you here, but now that you've written this insulting nonsense, I need to teach you a lesson. Then I'll let you get on with your miserable life." Turning to the soldier, he said, "Give him some cool water. He appears to be thirsty!"

Then he walked out the door. Several seconds later, two huge men walked in and dragged Dad to the basement. They put handcuffs on him and the interrogator reappeared. As he was being beaten and the taste of blood filled his mouth, he heard the interrogator tell the two men, "I still need his right hand." It was thus that they beat his entire left side with the handle of a shovel until he passed out.

He regained consciousness once as he was lying on the cement floor of a dark cell, his teeth chattering in the cold. The next day he awoke to find himself in a hospital bed, his left arm and one of his legs in a cast. He was too old to endure such agony and brokenness. His body was wracked with pain when a nurse arrived and injected him with painkillers, whereupon he fell into a deep sleep and dreamed about Sohrab, Beeta, and me. We were together in one cell. Sohrab had taken Dad's hands in his own and was kissing them, tearfully. Then he pointed to a small window near the ceiling and said, "The only way is to look at the sky. Sometimes birds fly by." Then Beeta caressed his wounded, broken feet and said, "The rest of the time, think of stories you heard as a child." I was hugging his shoulders from behind just the way he used to when showing me how to place my fingers to play the *tar*. I said, "Wait for me."

I really wanted Dad to know I would soon be coming to see him—whenever he willed it. I mean, as if it were possible to abandon an old man like this to the hands of *his* torturers? That's why, during the next interrogation, when the interrogator heard that Dad was prepared to summon my ghost to prove my existence, he froze. He gulped, gave a laugh, and tried to say in a voice devoid of fear, "Tell her to come then!" The words hadn't even fully left his mouth when I arrived. Turning off the light, I clawed at his body and tore his shirt. Then, I punched his face and flung him, along with his chair, against the wall.

I had no idea that I possessed such strength. I suppose it was hatred that gave it to me. The interrogator roared in terror and two armed guards rushed in. But they couldn't get the light switch to work. Finally, they turned on a torch and saw Dad sitting in his seat with a broken arm and leg, and the interrogator cowering in a corner with blood dripping from his cheek and back, his shirt in shreds.

That was the last time Dad saw that interrogator. The next interrogator was a broad-shouldered man of about forty with very short, cropped black hair. During their first meeting, as he was leafing through Dad's now very thick file, he said, "So you're in contact with ghosts and jinns. You know that in the Quran the punishment for sorcery is death. However, given your age, I'll offer you another chance. Here's a pen and paper. We spared your right hand so you could defend yourself— we're such good people! Now, write. But this time, tell the truth."

And with that, he left the room. Perhaps he was afraid if he stayed much longer I would attack him, too. Dad began to write. Again he wrote for days. Every day the interrogator would enter and read what Dad had written the day before, draw some questions out of it, note them down, and ask Dad to incorporate their answers into his memoirs.

Dad wrote everything again. This time he cut out all the parts he had realized were incomprehensible to their stale minds, and embellished here and there to make it thoroughly believable. This time he wrote nothing about the black snow or my ghost, or Aunt Turan joining the jinns, or Beeta and Issa's circular flames of love-making. In this new version, there was nothing about Homeyra Khatun's enchanted garden and well or Effat's black love, the magical sleep or Razan's holy fire—all of which I had told him about. He wrote nothing about the prayers of the ancient Zoroastrian priests or the mating of the cows and roosters with wild birds and animals during the time of the black snow. This time he wrote neither that Roza was once able to walk through the air above Naser Khosrow Street with *The Wayfarer* by Sohrab Sepehri, nor that his brother Khosrow could appear and disappear before everyone's eyes. Instead, he wrote that he had been completely opposed to the political system prior to his arrest, that Beeta had lost her sanity and now believed she had been transformed into a mermaid and was in a psychiatric ward; and that his wife, Roza, had Alzheimer's disease and had gone missing. He wrote that I had died in a fire Revolutionaries had lit in our house and they hadn't seen my body since. He wrote many things. Things that were partly his own dreams. He wrote that for years he suffered from depression and was house-bound until, one day, he set off and travelled through most of the country, teaching and procuring illicit political books for young people. He wrote that he was neither a monarchist nor a communist nor a Mojahedin; that he just wanted democracy and believed that people had the right to choose their religion, dress, and political parties, and that the media should be free. He wrote that he had no living family members and the story of his brother, Khosrow, had merely been a figment of this imagination; and that he had never had a sister by the name of Turan.

When he had finished, they read what he had written and

transferred him the following day directly to Evin Prison. He was never interrogated again, nor did he ever set foot in any court. He lived the next five years in prison imagining that one day someone would come to tell him his court date had arrived. Even after five years, six months, and ten days when—because of old age—he was released, he thought he would be taken to court to learn of the crimes with which he had been charged. They released him only after they were certain he had lost his mind and would die sooner or later, and that he posed no threat whatsoever to the Holy Islamic regime.

Dad had long since returned to his family home in Tehran when I dreamt that I was dreaming that he had died. Perhaps after all those years the time had come; I no longer needed Dad's permission. If Sohrab hadn't disappeared like that and if Beeta's fish-like mind allowed her to remember us, maybe we could have gathered together—as in years past—to sit around the fire and drink smoked tea; and listen to the lowing cows and bleating sheep. Perhaps we could have polished the grove's rusty lock and oiled its hinges; and pruned the trees, ploughed the earth and planted wheat, as in the olden days; or at least sat together on the porch and read a poem by Bizhan Jalali or Ahmad Shamlu.

Eventually, I decided to go and see Dad. He was alone in his bedroom and awake, but not surprised to see me. He was happy as we hadn't seen each other for years. I didn't need to see the wrinkles on his face and neck and his now completely grey hair and moustache to know that the time was near. Since his release from prison, he had done nothing but sit beside the window and stare at the courtyard. He didn't have much hair left. I was embarrassed that he still saw me as a thirteen-year-old girl while he, on the other hand, had aged so much in all these years. Perhaps it should be admitted that when I told him that Mom had been back home for a long time now, I expected him to quickly pack his bags and set off. But he just sat in the chair and let me sit beside him, in silence. He neither leapt up—his brittle bones wouldn't have allowed this anyway—nor did he gather his things. He didn't even insist I stay with him a bit longer. No! He merely asked me to drink tea with him.

CHAPTER 16

M om had returned and surprisingly took up her chores as if she'd never been away. The first day she cleared the dirt and dust from the shelves, books, and carpets with remarkable agility and, for the first time in years, entered her bedroom, evoking in her hazy memories. She poured a petrol and lime mix on the ants, opened the windows, and attacked the weeds and grasses that had nosily sprouted everywhere with a sickle. It was obvious she had learnt long ago how to stand up to life.

She went over to the pool Dad had made for his grandchildren and saw the fish, some of which had grown so much they were as long as the pool. There were so many that they were writhing around on top of each other. Although she was very happy to see me, it was clear she planned to punish herself by asking nothing. She wanted to torture herself every day, thinking about Beeta and Dad's fate and watching how the wrinkles in her face deepened. Even when she saw that the bathroom door had been cemented closed, its roof removed, and that the water lilies had grown out over the roof into the backyard and found their way to the pool, she didn't ask any questions.

In all of her suffering, I felt she had fundamentally changed. She was no longer that darling delicate, only daughter from Tehran that Dad only every spoke to with kindness. Now she was experienced, world-wise and tough; she let daily afflictions pass through her heart but didn't allow them to stop. Now it was her time to wait. Once she had taken care of everything in the house, had single-handedly built a new pool and transferred half the fish into it; once she had pulled and burned all the weeds in the entire five-hectare grove, and pruned the trees, she prepared herself for a long wait. She changed into clean clothes and sat on the porch with a cup of tea until on one of many days, in one year of many that lay ahead, Dad would arrive and she would say to him, "I would never have died before you came back, Hushang!"

The waiting took a very long time. Much longer than Mom had patience for or the grove, beset by weeds, could bear. Once again, the grove languished under unwanted growth and unpruned branches, while quietly continuing to exist; just like Mom between the kitchen, bedroom, and porch.

In the years of Mom's waiting in Razan, and Dad's in Evin Prison and Darband, on a foggy morning of an ordinary day when Mom had long since lost the fortitude and physical strength to tend to the grove and keep the house free of creeping vines, ants, and lizards; and the inhabitants of Razan had become used to war, black snow, and the absence of their sons and mothers; and the whole story of the First Soothsayer, Effat's black love, and Razan's holy fire had become mere distant, inconceivable memories; the brazen sound of chainsaws aroused the villagers from their sleep, once and for all. Behind the chainsaws, the lorries and trailers arrived and flattened the grasses and wild flowers, felled massive trees with trunks as big around as houses—and with them hundreds of dreams, and thousands of moments in the lives of all—loaded them up and carted them off to the city.

When the isolation and virginity of the village was so thoroughly violated overnight, the people were left wondering how they'd ended up in a game whose rules they hadn't written. The game of aggressor and victim. A game in which it didn't take long for the victims to become the aggressors, to become victim-aggressors. At the beginning, the villagers did what they could to survive the changes forced upon them by the chainsaws and all that came with them. But it wasn't long before they forgot their myths and dreams, their history and balance and, saws in hand, they themselves attacked the Hyrcanian forest, the forest entrusted to them by their ancestors. There was no longer any time of day or night when the sound of chainsaws, lorries, and trailers was not to be heard. They flagrantly rent the dreams of the forest and thousands of years of jinns and spirits. They dug up the graves of their Zoroastrian ancestors and looted their daily objects and jewelry, selling them as antiquities to low-level intelligence agents. In the depths of the forest they squashed the luminous blue butterflies under their new plastic boots freshly imported from the city, and the ringing of their mobile phones made the grasshoppers and butterflies take flight. The birds migrated, firefly larvae committed suicide in their eggs, and cicadas would not come out of their cocoons.

While the villagers thought that they had never been happier with their new, air-conditioned houses, mobile phones, vases full of plastic flowers, and shelves stocked with chips, Pepsi, and gum, Razan was collapsing at Roza's old feet and before her feeble eyes. And yet, if it hadn't been for Mom's timely shrewdness, profiteers would have attacked, thinking that our house, once again covered in moss, had been empty for years. They would have pillaged and murdered all the trees in the grove with their chainsaws.

The day that several people from the village and city came with their chainsaws and lorries and broke the rusty chain and lock on the gate to the grove, trampled the forget-me-nots and green and blue lizards, and cut down the old greengage trees as they went, it was Mom who sat up straight, grabbed the axe, went up to them, gave one of them a hard slap in the face, and said, "Take one more step, and I'll split you in two!" The villagers, led by Issa and thinking the family from Tehran who had inhabited this abandoned house had long since died or left, ran away at the sight of this old woman with long, grey, wild hair because they thought it must be ghosts that protected the house and land. Only Issa stood his ground. He took a step forward and in his local accent dared ask, "Ma'am, do you know Miss Beeta?" Mom had never seen Issa's sunburnt face, and so she turned around and walked away without answering. But Issa set off after her, and with his voice lost in the rustling of Mom's long dress as she walked through the grass, he said, "Please tell me. I have to see her."

Mom was sorely mistaken when she thought she could put them in their place with one slap. She didn't realize this was just the beginning. Children who, not too long ago, viewed with respect the family that had helped in the reconstruction of their homes and land after the one hundred-and-seventy-seven-day black snowfall, had now become aimless young and middle-aged men whose imported city laws allowed them to encroach on any "outsider" property. These laws, very belatedly and via Hossein who this time had returned to Razan with chainsaws, taught the villagers they could call rich people from Tehran "arrogant" and "Shah-sympathizers," and loot their belongings. It was thus that when rumors of Mom's presence in the big house spread, the harassment began.

A rabble of young people would gather around the house at night and throw stones at its pitched roof, break the windows, and recite obscene, sexual poems. Once in the middle of the night, five of the most foul came onto the porch and wanted the old woman to open the doors and sleep with them. Mom was furious and, for the first time in her whole life, she asked the Zoroastrian ghosts of the grove and her ancestors to come to her aid. Mom had not really put much hope in their help and so, when they arrived soon after, she shed tears of joy.

First, she hugged her mother whom she hadn't even dreamed about in years, and then together with her father, grandparents, me, and the Zoroastrian ghosts, we slowly opened the glass door and stepped out onto the porch. When the foul men saw us, they froze, and several wet their pants. Then, screaming and stumbling to the ground in their haste to get away, they ran. By the next day, rumors in Razan had it that the house was inhabited by ghosts. The ghosts didn't just save the house and grove that night from takeover and looting by the inhabitants of Razan who were running wild thanks to the cry for Islamic equality, but also prepared one of the best nights Mom had ever had. After the foul men had left, they pulled out chalices of wine, and together with the finest foods and meat, drank to each other's health, recounted memories, laughed, and danced until morning to an old record of Qamar that Mom found hidden behind a wardrobe.

After that night, Mom no longer felt lonely, and despite her God knows how many years, she straightened her back and gave a loud command to the ferns and fungus and grasses that poked up between the mosaic tiles throughout the house to retreat. She destroyed the ants and lizards, and it was clear she would do anything she could to stay alive until Dad arrived. She always remembered in time—but sometimes she would act as though she didn't recognize me at all. This didn't bode well, but I had promised myself I would stay to protect her from assault by creeping ferns, the cold, lizards, and men.

And yet, I believe it was Issa who saved Mom from a siege of memories, yearning, the *frrrt frrrt* of the creeping plants, and *rog rog* of the tree frogs who clung to the windows with their sticky feet. The day after the villagers had so obscenely attacked the grove with chainsaws, Mom awoke to the sound of a sickle cutting back the grass and weeds in slow, even movements, perhaps in an effort to find traces of the scorched circles of so many years ago, and saw Issa. She wanted to shoo him out with her cane, but before she could act, Issa said he had been the gardener there years before and now was willing to work for nothing to help the old lady of the house. Issa stayed for months, and with regret, remorse, and memories of his distant past with Beeta, he let the sickle, slowly, meditatively shear the grove, hoping perhaps to find a blackened stone as a souvenir of those years, underneath the thorns and thistles, and grass.

Mom got used to his presence and sometimes even took him tea or food, but she never spoke with him, leaving his enduring question unanswered. She didn't answer because she herself didn't know and was too proud to ask me, "Where is Beeta, really?"

Mom was sitting on the porch as she usually did, allowing the flies of routine to pass over her wrinkled skin but trying as much as possible to keep them from harming her heart. She was clutching a bunch of small pieces of paper and was looking intently at the words written on each of them. She hadn't found a place for some: love, dream, kiss, heartsickness, memory, sorrow, loneliness, fear, escape, infidelity, yearning, lovemaking, hope, anguish, desperation, death, God.

Objects in the house had been labelled with what remained of her memory. She taped a label on everything: the vase, table, books, refrigerator, paintings, paper. For several days, her mind was busy wondering where she should put "love" so she wouldn't forget it. She laughed at the thought of labelling the bed "love"! She thought, *It doesn't get more stupid than that.* Then for the first time she doubted a bit the order of the words. Words were moving around in her mind to form correct sentences. Maybe it would be more correct to think, *More doesn't it stupid get!* She looked again at the pieces of paper in her hand. Take this one: heartsickness. What should she stick "heartsickness" on? But it didn't take her more than a few moments to realize her problem was not just her memory, words, or names, but her sense of sentence structure had also become muddled. She wondered if she would even be able to express heartsickness if Hushang came back. Should she say, "Missed you I" or "You missed I"? Or perhaps it was enough just to say, "Missed." As she was playing with the pieces of paper in her hand, her philosophical understanding began to doubt the words in her head. She thought, *What ridiculous linguistic rules I've been dealing with all these years*, and as she verbalized it, she herself was surprised to hear, "I was ridiculous with language dealings in the rules of the year."

Mom got up, went inside the house and returned with a needle and thread. She sat down again in her usual chair. She took a look around to make sure I wasn't nearby. Then, with utter serenity, she slowly sewed each of the pieces of paper onto her long black dress. When she had finished, she took a deep breath and let the hot summer sun evaporate her remaining memory and carry it up to the sky. Together over her heart, she had sewn: love, heartsickness, lovemaking, sorrow, God, and hope.

And yet, on that beautiful sunny day, wrapped in the fragrance of secrets and dog-rose and wild primrose, as she sat there in the heat of the sun, fiddling with words and letting their melancholia sway in her head, her mind in a turbulent onrush of sleep and waking, consciousness and oblivion, she didn't know that a few minutes later Dad, old, shaking, and out of breath, would appear before her.

CHAPTER 17

One of the men standing at a distance and taking a video yelled, "Fuck her! Cool. I'll send it to everyone!"

The young man stopped trying to kiss Beeta, the helpless mermaid. Three other men came to help, twisting Beeta's arms tightly and holding them over her head so the young man could unzip his pants. Feeling around to find her vagina among the beautiful scales that shone silver like the moon in mid-cycle, with the other hand he pulled out his penis that had just swollen into a large erection. But no matter how much he groped and poked around with his fingers, he couldn't find anything. Curious and annoyed, he sat on Beeta and began examining and touching her. Finally, he jumped up and cried, "It doesn't even have a hole!"

For the last two hours, the locals had surrounded her and had been yelling, "Kill the mermaid, kill it!" Beeta, the mermaid who in the last few years had become younger and more beautiful by the day, had covered her naked breasts with her arms and long hair, and was cowering, terrified and trembling, as she looked into their greedy, animal eyes. The men had completely surrounded her so that she couldn't get away. One of them, wearing a Revolutionary Guard uniform and a long black moustache and beard, was pointing his gun at her, scowling deeply.

An old fisherman was dangling a fishhook with a brown worm attached to it over Beeta's head, laughing with rotten teeth and saying, "Eat it!" The hook and worm brushed against Beeta's mouth and laughed. Beeta turned away with revulsion and looked out at the sea from between the sweaty bodies of her attackers, the orange vendors, fisherman, and rice sellers. It was so close. Close enough that it would only take one jump and this nightmare would be over; and she would promise herself never, ever to set foot on dry land again, or make even the slightest effort to see us. Oh, what a mistake it had been to follow the dream she had had the night before, only to end up here. There was no trace of us left in her fish-like mind, but that accursed dream had suddenly brought everything back and she had come to the beach in the hope of seeing one of us, after all these years.

The yelling had increased again. More people had gathered around. Men had scrambled to park their tractors, motorcycles, trucks of citrus fruits and fish and rice—rushing over to watch. Those who were silent, those who perhaps didn't agree that she should be killed, pulled out their phones and began filming and taking photos with their calloused workers' hands. The few women who had stood with curiosity a little way back very quickly returned home because the men had told them, "It's a man thing." The rest kept shouting together, "Kill it! Kill it! It's a sign of the Last Days." Several people were bickering in the commotion. One was saying, "Why do you want to kill her? What did the poor thing do?"

"Can't you see she's naked?!"

"This one should be killed as a lesson to the rest. What if *they* want to come, too?"

The one who had dissented asked, "Which rest?"

"The rest of them . . . mythical creatures!"

The dissenter said, "She's real . . . What do you mean by 'mythical'? . . . Can't you see her?"

"Then where's she been all this time? What? Now demons and jinns and fairies are supposed to be real!"

Again, the dissenter insisted, "But come on! She didn't hurt anybody. We should talk to her."

Then, continuing to film, he pushed the others aside and, kneeling down next to the mermaid, said to the terrified Beeta, "What are you doing here?"

Seeing the compassion in his eyes, sobbing, Beeta wailed, "I just came to see my mother and father. That's all. If you let me go, I swear I'll leave and never come back!"

The men didn't understand anything. Although she easily understood human speech, for them her voice sounded something akin to a dolphin's. Somebody laughed and said, "What a funny voice she has." The man who was opposed to killing her didn't understand anything either, but out of pity he pretended he had. That's why he continued, "Is anyone else coming? I mean . . . any mythical creatures?"

Surprised, Beeta said, "Mythical creatures? How am I supposed to know? I just came to visit my family. I beg you, have mercy! Let me go home!"

No one heard anything but the dolphin-like sound and, yet again, the man asked, "What are their names? Tell me and we'll let you go."

Crying with anguish, Beeta dug her fingernails into her cheeks and screamed, "How am I supposed to know? I only know the fish and the merpeople. We live a long way away. Way over there." She waved her arm towards the other side of the Caspian Sea.

The young man looked in that direction and said, "I think she's trying to say the others are coming from the other side of the sea."

Horrified, a murmur rose from the men. But still the young man, turning to them, said, "Let her go. She didn't do anything."

One said, "Where? So she can go and tell the rest to come?"

Another said, "Oh, just think: one day you wake up and see mermaids, jinns, and spirits coming at us from the sea and forest. How awful!"

The other answered, "Security has become so bad! God protect us all."

Bewildered, Beeta looked at the men's mouths. One moment she was hopeful she would be released, the next moment, she was despairing, tired, dirty, covered in blood and crying. Her whole body hurt. She wanted them to leave her alone to cry and die on her own. She had been so foolish to think she could come to the beach and wait for us in broad daylight!

While the men were busy talking, she spotted a little corner of sea through their boot-clad feet. One jump was all it would take. Using every ounce of energy she had left, she jumped, slid on the sand through the muddy boots, and dragged herself towards the water; but the men saw, and grabbing her by the arms and shoulders and tail, threw her back into their midst.

Shoving the man who opposed her execution back, the other men moved in closer to the mermaid. They zoomed in on Beeta's firm, white breasts with their phones, on her back and her beautiful wavy tail. As he filmed, one young man said to the person standing next to him, "How cool! How beautiful!"

The other answered, "Look at her hair. Check out her round ass. I want some of that!"

The circle of people tightened. Eventually, someone came close enough to touch Beeta's shoulder. Feeling his hand become damp and slimy, he gave a loud laugh and said, "That's awesome! She's like fish!" He sniffed his hand and said, "Smells like fish too. Dead fish."

The others burst out laughing and came forward more boldly. They touched and squeezed her hair, her shoulders, her buttocks and breasts; laughing with yellow, tar-stained teeth and moustaches. Nobody was shouting, "Kill the mermaid!"

anymore. Gradually their hands became greedier, more aggressive. Beeta screamed and wept and tried to push their eager hands away. Finally, one of the youths grabbed both of her wrists and held them down on either side of her, forcing her to the ground where he lay on top of her.

Beeta screamed. She wailed. She yelled and pleaded for help. But her voice was incomprehensible to them. Laughing, the men said, "Her voice is like a dolphin. Cool! Are you filming? Take a video!"

The man who was lying on top of Beeta took her breasts in his mouth, sucking and biting greedily, but then suddenly spitting it out, saying with disgust, "Yuuck . . . she smells like slime and algae!" But he didn't leave her alone. He rubbed his face and chest into Beeta's firm, naked breasts and thrust his pelvis into her. He tried to find her mouth with his own to kiss her, suck her, but she fought constantly, turning her head from side to side, screaming and pleading.

When, giving up, the man angrily pulled himself off her, he said, "She doesn't have a hole!" The other men said with surprise, "What? How is that possible? How the fuck do they have babies?"

Someone else said, "Check again. You'll find it." Several other men came to help and Beeta, whose face and beautiful long black mer-hair was now matted with sand and mud, was turned this way and that as they groped under her buttocks and savagely stuck their fingers in her delicate fish-like skin. They didn't find a hole but her body had been wounded by the pressure of their fingers and nails. She bled. Screamed. Begged. The young man got up angrily and, zipping up his pants, kicked her hard in the side saying, "So what good are they?" Then, turning to the Guard with the gun, he yelled, "What are you waiting for?! Kill her!"

The young man who opposed her execution shook his head, sadly, as he filmed. He wanted to stop them, or at least say something, but looking at each of these locals he was reminded that he didn't stand a chance. He knew all of them, and they him. To several of them he owed money, he worked for another, and he wanted to ask for the hand of yet another's daughter. One was his mother's brother, and another an uncle on his father's side through marriage. In these small places where it seems people had lived together for thousands of years, everyone was somehow related. Secrets travelled by word of mouth and one person's whispers were all the talk at another's party. Taking a good look at each of their faces through the camera on his phone—all relatives near or far—he thought, for all of their external differences, their fights, divisions, gossip, and thinking themselves better than others, they were in fact a single spirit in several bodies. He thought of himself. He turned the camera towards himself. And who was *he* then? One of their children, the future father of some others of them. These thoughts saddened him and his hand trembled but he did not stop filming.

He turned the camera until it was on the face of the Guard. He zoomed in. The Guard was looking hesitantly at each of the men. He remembered that this man had been his religion teacher in high school and was his aunt's husband's neighbor. No one said anything, but a twinkle of consent and approval shone in all their eyes. Several people were smiling. In the end, someone shouted, "So what are you waiting for!" The others seemed to come out of a kind of collective daze, started to yell as one, "Kill her! Kill the mermaid!"

Just a few seconds later, the shot rang out; at the very moment, a seed of hope had germinated in the heart of the young man. He had had the idle, useless feeling that some otherworldly help would come to rescue her; but just several seconds later, he watched incredulously as Beeta, the beautiful mermaid, was killed with a forty-five caliber Colt pistol in front of dozens of witnesses. The Guard who did it smiled victoriously as he looked into the faces of each of the men, and then put the gun, still smoking from the barrel, back into its holster on his belt. Beeta's red blood flowed onto the hands and feet of the fishermen, and the orange and rice vendors. Some of those still filming sadly shook their heads, stopped filming, and left, whispering. Getting onto their motorcycles or into their cars, they hit the accelerator and sped away, hoping to be the first to post their videos on Instagram, Facebook and YouTube.

Two or three people who were standing there brought shovels from their cars and dug a hole right there in the sand and mud, and pushed Beeta into it with their feet, cursing as they did. "Slut! It wasn't for nothing she was killed! She must have done something!"

Several people who hadn't stopped filming, including the young man who was opposed to killing her, turned off their phones after getting detailed shots of the bullet hole in her chest and her blood on the sand that stretched to the sea and mixed with the salty Caspian waters, and, shaking their heads, sadly, left.

Those who remained, covered her grave with sand, shells and scallops so it would appear there was no body buried there at all. As the sun set, the last people walking along the shore went home to tell their wives the exciting story of what had happened, unaware that they had been informed several hours earlier by a little boy who had observed the whole thing.

They, the women, had gathered together and spoken about the tragedy. They despaired for hours. They cursed and condemned their husbands, their brothers and their fathers. But as darkness began to fall, each of them remembered the food on their stoves; remembered their children's still unfinished homework; remembered that if they weren't home on time, their husbands would be angry and yell at them; remembered the table-cloth that had to be already spread when their husbands arrived; that they had to pretend they knew nothing of what had happened so that there was even a chance their husbands would talk to them, confide in them, and feel again a closeness and intimacy that had long since disappeared from the relationship. Then they would drink a hot tea and go to bed together.

CHAPTER 18

D ad did return to Razan but not when I asked him to. He waited in Tehran for the mayor to come in person with the bulldozers to threaten and bribe them. Seeing that nothing had changed, the mayor gave in to the inevitable and asked Granddad, "Why are you willing to see the house destroyed, but not let me have it?" Granddad simply said, "Because you are destruction itself." Furious, the mayor gave the demolition order, and the workers who all blindly followed orders looted the whole house first, right before their incredulous eyes, loading even the smallest objects into their private cars and trucks, and carting it away. Granddad, Grandma, and Great Granddad, whose collective age was several hundred years, sat on the porch and watched as each and every carpet, rug, painting, statue, book, chandelier, old hinge, piece of painted china, historical crystal, copper and ceramic vessel containing a thousand memories was stolen. They saw how the workers handled their books and carelessly broke some old vases, frames, and dishes as they carried them away. They saw how they trampled the carpets and crushed the dog-rose trellis that had bloomed in that garden for two hundred years, under the wheels of their cars. They saw everything and said nothing. Destruction was total, and they did not have enough life left in them to change anything. Once the house had been emptied of every last object, the workers attacked the old carved windows and doors, removing them from the walls. Then, the last worker flagrantly lifted

Dad and the rest from the chairs they were sitting in and took the chairs, too. There was just one thing they didn't allow to be stolen: the old trunk from their great ancestor Zakariya Razi. Then, as planned, Dad, Granddad, Grandma, and Great Granddad embraced and kissed one another and, under the stunned gaze of the workers and mayor, Granddad, Grandma, and Great Granddad went into the inner veranda, took each other's wrinkled hands and sat down on the cement floor.

Dad didn't wait to see how the bulldozers demolished the house on the heads of his mother, father, and grandfather, burying them alive in their own home. He put the old trunk into the car and wept all the way to Razan.

CHAPTER 19

It was thus that even our great ancestor Zakariya Razi's prediction turned out to be wrong, and Beeta didn't live long enough to guard over the trunk and ancient books. How many times can someone absorb that final shot? It was the fourth time that life put Dad out of his misery. Beeta's brutal death was the last. With her death, the time for Mom and Dad to die had also arrived. I led them to where Beeta was buried. We pulled her out of the sand during the night, brought her to the grove, and among tears and lamenting, we dug a grave for her under an old oak tree. When we dug her grave and put in her beautiful, delicate body with that amazing tail, long hair, and scales that still shone in the early morning sun. We placed her ballet slippers in her hands and, beside her, the thousand-and-one-hundred-year-old family trunk containing two of Zakariya Razi's books, *The Prophets' Fraudulent Tricks* and *The Violation of Religion*. We covered it with earth and waited for the snow.

Seconds later, when snow began to fall, Sohrab and Beeta revealed themselves, enveloped in shining white flakes. We all hugged each other and smiled. We stood there and watched as the snow covered the whole grove. It covered the grave, the memories, the houses. We stood and watched as the snow covered all that had happened.

For the first time in years, all five of us were together, now. We held hands, and for a moment, we saw with open eyes the five-hectare grove in the future. We saw the house hidden and in ruins among ferns, trees, and grasses; the fish in the pool becoming so numerous they began eating each other; we saw that, for centuries, no one else built a wooden treehouse in the largest oak in the grove; and no one ever again reached enlightenment in the greengage tree. Nobody ever again felt excitement at seeing the crumbling fire temple or ancient Zoroastrian bones; and centuries later, when the grave of Beeta, the dejected mermaid, was discovered, journalists pounced and newspapers wrote that mermaids really had once existed. They could never understand, however, why she had a pair of pink ballet slippers in her hands and an ancient trunk with two handwritten books by Zakariya Razi at her side.

It was time. Under the soft and steady snowfall, out of respect for a lifetime of Mom and Dad's futile struggle and suffering, the trees, grasses, ferns, and honeysuckle vines twisted together, their stems pressed close, grew until the whole grove was concealed from outsiders under a green ceiling. We three siblings held hands exactly as we had when we were children and accompanied Mom and Dad into their bedroom, where they were going to die; though their death took much longer than any of us expected.

Mom and Dad kissed us calmly and serenely, then lay down next to each other on the bed, holding hands, eyes closed. Before dying, Mom said, "Soon we'll see you on the other side."

When, an hour later, they still hadn't died, smiling, Dad opened his eyes and said, "Death is slowly taking its course. You three get on with your own things." Then they both slipped quietly into a coma.

We left them and sat together in another room to wait. But waiting wasn't easy. Death still filled all of us with naïve fear and anxiety, and so we began reminiscing. We spoke about what we would do if we were alive, and what we would be doing if we had been born in another time or place. Beeta said she would surely have become a ballerina and fallen in love with an artist and married. Sohrab said he would have become a journalist, constantly travelling from country to country to get stories. I said that I would have liked to become a writer. Yet despite the fantasies, the fear of death still made its way between the lines of their words and memories and dreams, forcing itself on them. Beeta suddenly began to cry and said, "Mom and Dad deserved more than this. How did they manage the pain of seeing each of us die?"

Sohrab lit a cigarette and said, "Their lives can be summed up in two sentences: they fell in love with each other and wanted to build a beautiful future, but instead of a happy life for themselves and their children, they saw death, confusion, and suffering, and then died." I said, "I'm happy none of us had children! This isn't a safe world to bring children into."

Our anxiety increased by the moment, and the anger we felt as we talked about memories—each one worse than the one before—did not dissipate. One, two, three days passed, and our anguish did not disappear. It felt as though all our pain and suffering were collapsing down on top of us. Then, at sunset on the third day, a tired, dusty stranger with sad eyes and a large sack over his shoulder fought his way to the house through the bushes and trees and tangled vines of the grove. Entering the house without a greeting and as if he owned it, he went directly into Mom and Dad's bedroom, and then commanded loudly, "Come in here!" The three of us went. The sad-eyed stranger with prematurely grey hair said, "I have come with a message from your parents. They say they can't die until you've stopped your moaning and crying."

"How can we know you are telling the truth?" I said. With a calm expression, the man turned towards Mom and Dad who were still in a coma and commanded, "Sit up!" Then, moving as if not of their own volition, Mom and Dad's bodies sat up, their necks crooked. The man watched the three of us and when he saw we were convinced, he let the two lie down again.

He accompanied us out onto the porch and said, "They will die freely and meet you thirty minutes after your anger and anguish have ended." Then he left, just as he had come, disappearing among the trees and bushes.

It was thus that, in the middle of a cold winter night in one of God's many years, Mom and Dad died and joined us, as we sat around a fire in the courtyard. At daybreak the next morning, when the last of the fire's embers were extinguished, Mom got up and walked towards the forest in silence, and not knowing where we were going, we followed. We walked and walked until we reached a greengage tree and stopped. Its branches were still laden with greengage plums. We picked a few and ate them. It was the last flavor that we were to take with us from this world. "Strange that I'd never seen this tree before," I mused. "That's because it's a tree, just like any other," Mom replied as she began to climb. The four of us followed. The tree wasn't very large and it seemed unlikely it could hold the weight of all five of us; but it wasn't long before we realized that it became taller and stronger as we climbed. After several meters, we stopped and so, too, did the tree's growth. When we continued to climb upwards, so did the tree. We climbed and climbed until we passed the clouds and could see Planet Earth below us. For a moment, we stopped, and so did the tree. We looked down. Down at Earth with all its forests, its oceans, mountains, and clouds; with all its countries, borders, people, loves, hates, murders, and pillaging. We looked at each other and realized how easy it was for us to let go now. We continued our ascent until we reached the very top of the tree. Mom, who was furthest up, turned and looked at each of us, then smiled, and was suddenly absorbed into the bark, and disappeared. Next Dad, then Sohrab, Beeta, and then finally me. That's it.

Acknowledgments

I would like to thank my father for teaching me to fly in the sky of literature freely. I owe a debt of gratitude to my mother, without whose support I would not be living in the free country of Australia, able to write without censorship.

I am profoundly grateful to the Australian people for accepting me into this safe and democratic country where I have the freedom to write this book, a liberty denied me in my homeland.